Zen Past and Present

Key Issues in Asian Studies, No. 8

AAS Resources for Teaching About Asia

ZEN PAST AND PRESENT

ERIC CUNNINGHAM

Association for Asian Studies, Inc.
825 Victors Way, Suite 310
Ann Arbor, MI 48108 USA
www.asian-studies.org

KEY ISSUES IN ASIAN STUDIES
A series edited by Lucien Ellington, University of Tennessee at Chattanooga

"Key Issues" booklets complement the Association for Asian Studies' teaching journal, *Education About Asia*—a practical teaching resource for secondary school, college, and university instructors, as well as an invaluable source of information for students, scholars, libraries, and anyone with an interest in Asia.

Formed in 1941, the Association for Asian Studies (AAS)—the largest society of its kind, with close to 8,000 members worldwide—is a scholarly, non-political, non-profit professional association open to all persons interested in Asia.

For further information, please visit www.asian-studies.org

For orders or inquiries, please contact:
    Association for Asian Studies, Inc.
    825 Victors Way, Suite 310
    Ann Arbor, MI 48108 USA
    Tel: (734) 665-2490; Fax: (734) 665-3801
    www.asian-studies.org

Library of Congress Cataloging-in-Publication Data

Cunningham, Eric, 1962–

  Zen past and present / Eric Cunningham.
      p. cm. — (Key issues in Asian studies ; No. 8)
      (AAS resources for teaching about Asia)
  Includes bibliographical references.

  ISBN 978-0-924304-64-4 (pbk. : alk. paper) 1. Zen Buddhism—History.
  I. Title.
  BQ9262.3.C86 2011
  294.3'92709—dc23

                                                                    2011033128

*To my friend, mentor
and Shining
Beacon of The Dharma,
Mark Unno*

ABOUT "KEY ISSUES IN ASIAN STUDIES"

Key Issues in Asian Studies (KIAS) is a series of booklets engaging major cultural and historical themes in the Asian experience. *KIAS* booklets complement the Association for Asian Studies' teaching journal, *Education About Asia*, and serve as vital educational materials that are both accessible and affordable for classroom use.

"Key Issues" booklets tackle broad subjects or major events in an introductory but compelling style appropriate for survey courses. Although authors of the series have distinguished themselves as scholars as well as teachers, the prose style employed in *KIAS* booklets is accessible for broad audiences. This series is particularly intended for teachers and undergraduates at two- and four-year colleges as well as advanced high school students and secondary school teachers engaged in teaching Asian studies in a comparative framework and anyone with an interest in Asia.

For further information about *Key Issues in Asian Studies* booklets, *Education About Asia*, or the Association for Asian Studies, visit www.asian-studies.org.

Prospective authors interested in *Key Issues in Asian Studies* or *Education About Asia* are encouraged to contact:

> Lucien Ellington
> University of Tennessee at Chattanooga
> Tel: (423) 425-2118
> Fax (423) 425-5441
> E-Mail: Lucien-Ellington@utc.edu
> www.asian-studies.org/EAA

"Key Issues" booklets available from AAS:

> *Japan and Imperialism, 1853–1945* by James L. Huffman
>
> *Japanese Popular Culture and Globalization* by William M. Tsutsui
>
> *Global India circa 100 CE: South Asia in Early World History*
> by Richard H. Davis
>
> *Caste in India* by Diane Mines
>
> *Understanding East Asia's Economic "Miracles"* by Zhiqun Zhu
>
> *Political Rights in Post-Mao China* by Merle Goldman
>
> *Gender, Sexuality, and Body Politics in Modern Asia* by Michael Peletz

About the Author

Eric Cunningham, Associate Professor of History, has been the East Asian historian at Gonzaga University since 2003. A specialist in modern Japanese intellectual history, he received an MA in modern Japanese literature from the University of Oregon in 1999, and a PhD in history from the same institution in 2004. Cunningham's research interests include Japanese intellectual, Zen Buddhism, Catholicism, psychedelia, and eschatology. He is the author of *Hallucinating the End of History: Nishida, Zen, and the Psychedelic Eschaton* (Academica Press, 2007).

CONTENTS

Acknowledgments

The people who were instrumental in fostering my appreciation for Zen, and for guiding my understanding of its richness over the years are too numerous to name or even remember. I would like though, to recognize a few people who have helped me enter the scholarly conversation on Zen—in particular Jeffrey Barlow, the brilliant long-time editor of the E-ASPAC online journal. I would also like to acknowledge the great people at the Association for Asian Studies, in particular Lucien Ellington, Jonathan Wilson and Gudrun Patton who have been so warm and encouraging throughout the process of bringing this booklet to life. Finally, I would like to thank my students, past and present, who year-in and year-out remind me of how exciting it was to encounter Zen for the first time, and allow me to share in the enthusiasm of their own discovery.

Editor's Introduction

Zen, if for no other reason, probably deserves to be a *Key Issues* topic because it is virtually impossible to be literate and not encounter the word on a regular basis in the U.S. and most other Western countries. Zen has been associated with everything from perfume to sports, movies, and the so-called "New Age" movement. Anyone who asks a group of 19-year-old undergraduates can be assured that a substantial number of them will have at least heard the term "Zen." What exactly is Zen? How and why did a belief system predicated on the assertion that words are not the answer, spread first through many Asian cultures and ultimately to the West as well? In what follows, Eric Cunningham does a superb job of enabling students—and those of us who teach them as well—to get a handle on these two questions.

Cunningham, an historian who has both personal and academic interests in Zen, is also an engaging writer with a good sense of humor. The author first poses variants of the questions I mentioned in a well-crafted introduction. He then explores Zen's Buddhist roots and subsequent traditions, and how they were transmitted throughout East Asia. Eric tells Zen's story well in several respects as readers will gain a good understanding of Zen's history, the fundamental tenets of major Zen sects and of the belief system's influence on premodern East Asia, particularly Japan. Cunningham then explores Zen's changing role in the Japan of the Meiji and Shōwa eras and chronicles its transmission to the West and subsequent transformation into a high profile popular cultural phenomenon. He does all this in prose that is highly accessible for a general audience.

This *Key Issues* booklet would not have been possible without the work of several people. First and foremost, working with Eric Cunningham was a pleasure. Thanks also go to Steve Heine who read the initial proposal and to Hal French and William Londo who provided excellent specific suggestions on the completed manuscript. As the number and variety of our *Key Issues* series increases, I am as always deeply grateful to the AAS Editorial Board, AAS Publications Manager, Jonathan Wilson, and AAS Publications Coordinator, Gudrun Patton, for their strong support of pedagogy as evidenced by such projects as *Key Issues in Asian Studies* and *Education About Asia*.

Lucien Ellington
Series Editor, Key Issues in Asian Studies

Timeline

589 BCE: The awakening of Siddartha Gautama (560–480 BCE) as the historical Buddha.

390 BCE: A split emerges in the Buddhist monastic community between the Theravada elders and the proponents of what will become the Mahāyāna (Greater Vehicle) school.

First century BCE: Buddhist missionaries begin traveling to China.

150–250 CE: The Mahāyāna priest Nagarjuna develops the philosophy of *prajñāpāramitā*, "perfected wisdom"

ca. 400 CE: The Indian-Kuchean monk Kumārajīva (344–413) translates essential Mahāyāna texts into Chinese.

ca. 520: The Indian monk Bodhidharma (470–543), the twenty-eighth patriarch of Buddhism and first patriarch of Zen, establishes the Chan (Zen) tradition in China.

ca. 700: Under the sixth patriarch, Huineng (638–713), the Chan sect separates into the northern and southern sects. The southern sect is known for favoring the path of "sudden enlightenment." The northern sect disappears within a few generations.

845: Following severe imperial persecutions of Buddhism in China, only the Chan sect survives intact.

ca. 850: The southern sect breaks into the "Five Schools" of Chan Buddhism. Of these five, only the Linji (Rinzai) and Caodong (Sōtō) will remain as distinct schools in subsequent centuries.

960–1279: The Song dynasty, a period in which Chan poets and ink painters establish a new aesthetic standard in Chinese art.

1191: The Rinzai Zen sect is established in Japan by the monk Eisai (1141–1215) during the Kamakura period (1185–1333).

1227: The Sōtō Zen sect is established in Japan by the monk Dōgen (1200–1253).

1341: First official ranking of the *gozan* (Five Mountain) temple system in Japan.

1333–1573: Japan's Muromachi era is considered by many to be the golden age of Japanese Zen thanks to the active patronage of the Ashikaga shogunate.

1600–1868: Japan's Tokugawa era, a long period in which Buddhism survives, although it loses the active support of the government.

1661: The Ōbaku Zen sect is established in Japan.

1868–1912: The Meiji era of Japan, in which Zen returns to prominence.

1893: The Rinzai abbot Shaku Sōen introduces Zen to the West at the World Parliament of Religions in Chicago.

1895–1945: Zen is drawn into the construction of Japanese "cultural nationalism," which dominates Japanese consciousness until the end of World War II.

1897: D. T. Suzuki (1870–1966) begins his career in America as the "Zen apostle to the West," living and working in La Salle, IL, before returning to Japan in 1909.

1949: D. T. Suzuki returns to the United States, helping to initiate a "Zen boom" there.

ca. 1966–present: In the wake of the initial Zen boom, Zen continues to influence both academic scholarship and popular culture in the modern Western world.

1

WHAT IS ZEN?

The word *Zen* has the power to evoke certain pictures in the modern mind. It may present to our imaginations scenes of Japanese monks meditating in the stillness of mountain temples in medieval Kyoto or samurai warriors pondering the impermanence of life as they share a bowl of tea on the eve of battle. The word can conjure up more contemporary images, too, many in which westerners themselves play the role of the Zen adept. We see Eugen Herrigel, the German professor who found "enlightenment" while studying Japanese archery in the 1920s. Or "dharma bum" Jack Kerouac, whose search for the Buddha took him from the taverns of San Francisco to the peaks of the Sierras in the 1950s. We also have the "lone wolf," Phaedrus, of *Zen and the Art of Motorcycle Maintenance* fame, whose struggle to resolve the conflict between romance and reason on a road trip through the western states became a touchstone of American cultural literacy in the 1970s. Of the many exports Japan has sent abroad during the modern age, perhaps none has become more embedded in the Western imagination than Zen, although it is probably safe to say that most westerners would be hard-pressed to define Zen in any satisfactory way. Whether it is simply a property inherent to the "inscrutability" of Zen or a consequence of incomplete cultural adoption, our understanding of Zen, while rich in imagery, is rather poor in articulation.

If asked to give a definition of *Zen*, most of us would be able to say that it has something to do with Japanese Buddhism. Many would say (because they may have once purchased a tabletop Zen garden kit) that it has something to do with nature, however artificially stylized. Others might say (if they read *Zen and the Art of Motorcycle Maintenance*) that it has something to do with transcending duality. Still others might suggest (having followed Bart Simpson's path to enlightenment while training for a miniature golf tournament) that it possesses a paradoxical wisdom, conveyed through riddles called *kōan*. Finally, some would know (remembering what they read about basketball legend Phil Jackson's theories of coaching in *Sports Illustrated*) that it helps athletes optimize their performance by allowing them to break through mental blocks and "go with the flow." The whole Zen "thing" seems to exist in a cloud of image and intuition, and coming up with a concrete definition presents a difficult challenge. As the Zen scholar Alan Watts once wrote, "Zen is above all an experience, nonverbal in character, which is simply inaccessible to the purely literary and scholarly approach."[1]

Well, if Zen is so "nonverbal" and "inaccessible" to the literary approach, why in the world are there so many books written about it? In my own thirty-year association with Zen, spanning a phase of youthful infatuation all the way to my present state of middle-aged appreciation, I have read hundreds of books and articles on the topic, skimmed several hundred more, and probably ignored several thousand. The number of books published since the so-called Zen boom of the 1950s and 1960s has been remarkable, with no letup in recent decades, even though the boom years are long past. Browsing in any large bookstore, or surfing the Internet, one can find a mind-boggling variety of books and websites related to Zen, relatively few of which offer any sustained treatment of Buddhism. A curious reader can find books on Zen gardening, Zen cooking, Zen fighting, Zen driving, Zen real estate, Zen fashion, Zen investing, Zen office management, Zen golfing, Zen fishing, Zen child rearing—and this is only the beginning. There would seem to be a "Zen way" to cultivate any taste, hobby, profession, or lifestyle. Because my own research covers religion, Japanese philosophy, and cultural history, I have had the occasion to collect many of these works over the years and have been much entertained (if not always greatly edified) in seeing how Zen is appropriated and reappropriated according to changing commercial trends.

Among the more interesting Zen books is a pocket-sized compendium of wisdom called *The Little Zen Companion*, which has enjoyed robust sales since its publication in 1994. Editor David Schiller admits that his book is not an analysis of Buddhism and does not even "presume to define *Zen*," but it obviously owes its popularity to the implied promise that it offers some kind of Zen wisdom. Unfortunately, a reader trying to pin down the meaning of *Zen* with the *Companion* may find it more confusing than clarifying. Interspersed with random comments from authentic "Zen masters," are aphorisms such as these.[2]

> The eye with which I see God is the same eye with which God sees me. (Meister Eckhardt)

> I'm astounded by people who want to "know" the universe when it's hard enough to find your way around Chinatown. (Woody Allen)

The true value of a human being can be found in the degree to which he has attained liberation from himself. (Albert Einstein)

Life and love are life and love. A bunch of violets is a bunch of violets, and to drag in the idea of a point is to ruin everything. Live and let live. Love and let love, flower and fade, and follow the natural curve, which flows on, pointless. (D. H. Lawrence)

None of these quoted "masters" was ever a practicing Zen Buddhist and none was consciously trying to capture the essence of Zen in any of these quotes. Why, then, are these comments considered to be "Zen"? After thumbing through the *Companion*, one might conclude that Zen is a way to express irony or convey pithy homespun wisdom. A more reflective reader might think that Zen is some kind of religious ideal, pointing to a reality that lies beneath the appearances of the everyday world. In either case, one would be partially right, but why is *that* necessarily Zen? Any religious or philosophical tradition can offer us these things. What is it, exactly, that makes a Zen thing Zen? Is it all a trick? Is it just a marketing gimmick? Whatever attraction it may hold for the earnest consumer of wisdom, the word *Zen* leaves a good deal unanswered when it comes to defining itself.

The student looking for a good, rigorous definition of *Zen* is not helped by the fact that "certified" Zen masters have always been notorious for claiming that *Zen* is simply impossible to define. Zen scholar Abe Masao observes:

It is clear that Zen is not a philosophy. It is beyond words and intellect and is not, as in the case of philosophy, a study of the processes governing thought and conduct, nor a theory of principles or laws that regulate people and the universe. For the realization of Zen, *practice is absolutely necessary.*[3]

Daisetsu Teitaro (D. T.) Suzuki (1870–1966), a man widely recognized as the most important figure in modern Zen, is similarly evasive in his definition of it. This is remarkable considering the fact that Suzuki made it his life's work to explain Zen to the Western world. In an astonishingly fruitful seventy-year career, Suzuki translated many of the "canonical" Zen texts into English and personally taught several generations of Western devotees both the esoteric profundities and practical applications of the Zen life. It would seem that a scholar fluent in several languages, with hundreds of books, articles, and translations to his credit, would be able to articulate a lucid definition of *Zen*. Unfortunately, his long characterization of Zen from the classic *Essentials of Zen Buddhism* follows the fairly common technique of explaining what Zen *is* through a series of statements describing what Zen *is not*.

"Is Zen a system of philosophy?" Suzuki asks. *Not really.* Is Zen a form of Buddhism? *Not exactly.* Is Zen a religion? *Not entirely.* "The truth," Suzuki assures us, is that "Zen is extremely elusive as far as its outward aspects are concerned."

> When you think you have caught a glimpse of it, it is no more there; from afar it looks approachable, but as soon as you come near it, you see it even farther away from you than before. Unless therefore, you devote some years of earnest study to the understanding of its primary principles, it is not to be expected that you begin to have a fair grasp of Zen.[4]

It would appear, then, that Zen cannot be clearly understood or even *approached*, yet, somehow, as Suzuki also tells us, it contains the essence of "all the philosophy, religion, and life itself of the Far Eastern peoples."[5] Even a logic-bound westerner can grasp the idea that certain things—love, joy, and sorrow, certainly—are better apprehended through experience than through intellect, but how can we accept that anything so vague could constitute the core of an entire civilization? Perhaps it is true that Zen cannot be understood but only lived—but if that is true, how do we account for the profusion of books, journals, recordings, documentaries, and websites that try to explain it, to say nothing of the profusion of manufactured goods that allow us to purchase Zen as if it were a consumer commodity? There is clearly something far-reaching and profound taking place in that cultural domain called Zen, but Zen is not telling us what it is.

The purpose of this booklet is to provide a concise understanding of Zen for the reader who has had no exposure to it and may not be in a position to practice it. As scandalous as it may sound to the Zen purist, we can define *Zen*; we can study its history, we can analyze its logic, and we can measure the range of its effects. Profundity and paradox notwithstanding, there remains a great deal we can say about Zen. My approach to this topic, as the title suggests, will be historical. By locating the time and place of its origin, and tracing its development in the historical world, we can identify an adequate set of defining criteria that will allow us to speak confidently about Zen. This, I believe, will not only add to our objective knowledge but enrich our subjective appreciation of this fascinating element of Asian civilization. As an historical study, this booklet employs a variety of interpretive approaches. We will look at the religious, philosophical, political, cultural, and aesthetic components of Zen, and we will proceed not by discussing what Zen is *not*, but by focusing on the many things Zen *is* and has been throughout its long and fascinating history. I trust that readers will acquire both a good historical understanding of and a well-informed critical respect for Zen Buddhism.

Let us return to the original question, then, and propose a basic, working definition of *Zen*. We can begin simply by saying that *Zen* is the Japanese rendering of the Chinese word *chan*, which is the Chinese rendering of the Sanskrit word *dhyāna*, which refers to the state of meditation. In the most literal sense, Zen is meditation. When people refer to Zen Buddhism, they are referring to that particular sect of the Buddhist Mahāyāna tradition whose adherents seek enlightenment through meditation. This is clear enough to serve as a starting point. Obviously meditation is not the totality of Zen practice, and it does not exhaust the meaning of Zen as a historical phenomenon, but there is no reason that Zen should be any more indefinable than anything else we study. By starting with this simplest of definitions, we will discover that Zen did not begin as a fully formed abstraction describing both everything and nothing, but rather as a specific practice (meditation) in a specific spiritual tradition (Buddhism), with a very specific historical origin (the enlightenment of the Buddha). If we want to understand how Beat poetry, Japanese archery, the tea ceremony, or motorcycle maintenance all share some common property called Zen, then we ought to start by looking at what Zen meant to its first and most remarkable master.

2

THE BUDDHA'S OWN ZEN

The only way we can really understand the global phenomenon we call Zen is to look at its historical roots in Indian Buddhism and recognize the central role that *dhyāna*, or "meditation," played in the original awakening of the Buddha. The historical Buddha, a prince named Siddartha Gautama, permanently altered world history and human consciousness when, in the middle of the sixth century BCE, he attained enlightenment while meditating under a bodhi tree. His *samadhi* (in Japanese, *satori*, "awakening") was the culmination of over seven years of striving to find a way to understand and transcend human suffering.

According to numerous legends of the Buddha's life compiled after his passing, Gautama was destined to lead humanity on the path to enlightenment. His birth was a miraculous event, containing certain parallels to the familiar story of the birth of Christ, in which a divine being participates in his own conception. As the story goes, one day Queen Maha-Maya was resting on a couch when the Buddha appeared as a white elephant beside her.[1] Trumpeting three times, the elephant entered the queen's side, causing her to conceive a son. Ten months later, at the celebration of the child's birth, a wandering mendicant named Asita prophesied that the boy would grow up and encounter a decrepit man, a sick man, a dead man, and a monk. On seeing these four signs, Asita predicted that Gautama would renounce the world and his throne and take up the life of a holy man. The king was alarmed at this prophecy, and decided to keep his son sequestered in the palace, making sure he was denied no necessity or pleasure, and exposed to no unpleasant sights of the outside world. Nevertheless, near the age of thirty, while riding in a carriage outside the palace, Gautama did see each of the people predicted by Asita, and after some days of troubled pondering on the phenomenon of human suffering, he decided to leave home and take up the life of an ascetic. His goal was to discover the cause of human suffering and to attain the means of overcoming it.

In the early phase of his vocation, Gautama followed the path of renunciation. He became the pupil of several hermit teachers, or *sramana*, who taught him the techniques of fasting, celibacy, meditation, and the discipline of his appetites. After seven years of self-denial, he came to realize that none of the hardships he experienced had brought him any closer to an understanding of the problem of suffering. Despite his heroic mortifications of the spirit and flesh, true enlightenment continued to elude him. Gautama finally abandoned the severe fasting that had brought him close to the point of death, but he continued to meditate in the forests, often throughout the night, in order to attain the calm and internal quiet that he hoped would lead him to liberation. One night, tradition tells us, while sitting under the fabled bodhi tree (a kind of fig), and resolving not to move until he had attained enlightenment, he was assailed by a demon named Mara, who promised earthly power and pleasure if only he would agree to abandon his path. Gautama refused to submit to Mara's temptations and prevailed in his *dhyāna*, ultimately forcing the demon to flee. At dawn, with the first sight of the morning star, Gautama experienced his awakening to Buddhahood, attaining perfect knowledge of birth, death, and the meaning of suffering.

Figure 2.1. The Buddha in Sitting Meditation. Sarnath Museum (Dhammajak Mutra), India.

In his first public sermon after enlightenment, a talk called "Setting in Motion the Wheel of the Dharma," the Buddha explained what he called the Four Noble Truths. The first noble truth is the truth of *suffering*, the insight that life and all of its processes are based on suffering. Birth leads to death, desire leads to more desire, and material wants are never satisfied. The second noble truth is that *desire is the origin of all suffering*. The third noble truth is that *suffering can end only through the cessation of desire*. The fourth noble truth describes the means by which desire can be overcome, a way of life called the *Noble Eightfold Path*. The Noble Eightfold Path is a sustained practice of integrated self-disciplines designed to liberate the seeker from the suffering caused by earthly life. It represents the means by which a person can become free of endless birth and rebirth and extinguish the candle of existence through the attainment of nirvana. The Eightfold Path consists of:

1. Right view or right belief
2. Right resolution or right intention
3. Right speech
4. Right action
5. Right livelihood or right work
6. Right endeavor or right effort
7. Right thought or mindfulness
8. Right concentration, or meditation

Considered in light of the many philosophies, artifacts, belief systems, and practices that Buddhism has generated over the last twenty-five hundred years, the Four Noble Truths and the Noble Eightfold Path seem to be a rather sparse foundation. Nevertheless, they were the core of a refreshing new dharma of human consciousness, which is to say, a "doctrine" or "law" that spread through northern India with revolutionary effect.[2] For the next forty-five years, the Buddha and his yellow-robed disciples wandered through the Ganges River valley preaching the *madhyamika,* or "middle way," between self-indulgence and asceticism. This teaching set the Buddha apart from the other *sramana* of his day, as he rejected the intense fasting and mortifications that these teachers believed were necessary for the renunciation of worldly attachment. The Buddha also rejected the traditional Brahmanic priesthood, criticizing both the caste system and the traditional teaching that Brahma, the supreme and holy essence of the universe, was accessible only to the priestly class. A man did not come to Brahma by virtue of his family or birth, the Buddha insisted, but through the attainment of truth and righteousness. By the time the Buddha attained *parinirvana* in approximately 483 BCE, the Buddhist community, or *sangha*, had grown to include hundreds of disciples and had produced a rich canon of scriptures and commentaries.

When the Buddha departed the world, he left no specific instructions for his followers other than to encourage them to be their own lamps in the quest for enlightenment. Tradition holds that his "successor" (a designation that would refer only to his position as patriarch of the community, certainly not to any inherited status as Buddha) was Mahākāsyapa, a monk who holds a special place in the hearts of Zen Buddhists. According to a legend (which may actually have been invented centuries later by Chinese *chan* monks), Mahākāsyapa was selected because he alone among the disciples seemed to understand and appreciate an unexpected gesture made by the Buddha during the so-called Flower Sermon.

As the legend is told, the Buddha was nearing the end of his life and wanted to give his disciples some final instruction. He assembled them by the side of a lake and began to teach. In this particular sermon, though, the Buddha uttered no words. Instead, he held up a lotus flower and showed it to each of his disciples in turn, each of whom became confused as they attempted to explain what it meant. At last the Buddha came to Mahākāsyapa, who looked at the flower, smiled, and began to laugh. With this, the Buddha handed the flower to him, and said:

> I have the all-pervading True Dharma, incomparable Nirvana, exquisite teaching of formless form. It does not rely on letters and is transmitted outside scriptures. I now hand it to Maha Kasho [Mahākāsyapa].[3]

The Zen sect's high regard for the Flower Sermon comes, as we will see later, from its apparent validation of "instant enlightenment" and the possibility of wordless transmission of the dharma. Mahākāsyapa did not have to demonstrate great knowledge of scripture or any prodigies of asceticism to gain the Buddha's stamp of approval. He simply "understood," with silent and loving good humor, an attitude that has long been an ideal characteristic of Zen spirituality. Our knowledge of the Buddha's "official" sayings and deeds comes from a remarkable collection of scriptures known as the Tripitaka (the three baskets). The first of these is the Vinaya Pitaka, the "basket of discipline," which contains the rules and requirements of monastic life. The second is the Sutra Pitaka, the "basket of teachings," a vast collection of discourses of varying lengths concerning doctrine and conduct. The third is the Abhidharma Pitaka, the "basket of metaphysics." This is a miscellaneous collection of writings that elaborate or illustrate the teachings of various sutras.

These texts, known collectively as the Pali Canon, were compiled by his chief disciples, a group of men who became known to history as "the elders" or Theravadin. As men who were handpicked by the Buddha, and had known him personally, they were accorded a high level of respect in the first several generations after the foundation of Buddhism and assumed authority over the propagation of the dharma. The Buddhism of the elders was (and is) considered an orthodox strain, focusing on the Four Noble Truths and a philosophical belief in the impermanence of life. Its followers seek nirvana, or "extinction," through meditation and poverty, and they value monastic community life as the ideal environment for following the dharma. The elders, in their attempt to preserve what they believed were the true doctrine and authentic lifestyle of the Buddha, regularized their practice into what is known today as the Theravada school of Buddhism.

In contrast to the orthodoxy of the Theravada, other disciples came to call themselves Mahāyāna, or "Greater Vehicle," Buddhists, inasmuch as their doctrine became more metaphysical and more open to the possibility of the attainment of salvation for believers—as opposed to merely the "blowing out" of existence through entering nirvana. In one sense then, where human ends are concerned, we might say that the chief difference between the Theravada and Mahāyāna schools is that the Theravada favors the annihilation of suffering through the attainment of nirvana and the Mahāyāna seeks the transcendence of suffering through the attainment of a supernatural state, relying on the assistance and intercession of a plethora of exalted beings

As the Mahāyāna school grew, it also gave birth to a great many new doctrines, teachings, theologies, and aesthetic forms that were not accepted by Theravada Buddhists—a fact that has encouraged many scholars over the years to suggest that Mahāyāna emerged as a lay-based, more "democratized" school than the elitist and monastic Theravada. While it is true that Mahāyāna Buddhists constitute the great majority of practicing Buddhists in the world, historical evidence does not support the argument that the Mahāyāna school was any kind of lay or populist movement. It seems plausible that its metaphysical leanings were influenced by the philosophies of Persia and Greece, whose armies invaded India in the sixth and fourth centuries BCE, and its precepts appealed to a wide spectrum of believers, but it did not begin as a lay movement. The early Mahāyāna sects were hierarchical, monastic, and ascetic, and they made no alterations to the Four Noble Truths or the Eightfold Path.

Mahāyāna Buddhism is undeniably more encompassing than Theravada Buddhism, which is sometimes, though usually inaccurately, called Hinayana, or the "Lesser Vehicle." There is no denying that the Mahāyāna faith opened Buddhism to new doctrinal and aesthetic possibilities. Perhaps the most significant doctrinal addition was the concept of the *boddhisattava*, or "Buddha-to-be," a term that refers to saintly personages who postpone their attainment of Buddhahood, choosing instead to remain in the world in order to save sentient beings. The greatest aesthetic innovations can be seen in the veneration of pictorial and sculptural images of the Buddha, which accompanied a tendency to regard the Buddha as a god in heaven rather than merely a human who had attained nirvana.

We will take a closer look at the theological and philosophical developments of Mahāyāna Buddhism in upcoming chapters. For now the point I want to stress concerning the Theravada-Mahāyāna split is that as Buddhism began to move into new doctrinal and devotional territory, it became attractive to more and more people, and its adoptees increasingly cut across caste lines. Buddhism rapidly grew from a religion of monks to a religion of the people and their rulers. Both commoners and kings found that Buddhism offered meaningful answers to real-life concerns. For commoners, Mahāyāna Buddhism offered a fresh moral perspective on life, liberation from rigid social categories, and the promise of salvation. For rulers, it provided a means of articulating political legitimacy, appealing as it did to absolute authority, and universal truth. The emperor Asoka (300–232 BCE), who converted to Buddhism around 264, did so out of remorse for the suffering he had caused during his bloody campaigns to unify India. As the self-proclaimed protector of the dharma, Asoka commissioned the building of stupas and prayer pillars throughout his empire, structures that concretely marked and proclaimed the universal ideals that united the emperor and his subjects to the Buddha dharma.

Asoka's determination to spread Buddhism to neighboring lands gave impetus to the first missionary excursions beyond India. Buddhist missions followed two broad vectors of transmission, a sea route through the Indian Ocean toward Southeast Asia and an overland route across the Asian continent. As a general rule, Theravada monks went to Southeast Asia, establishing communities in Ceylon (Sri Lanka), Burma, Thailand, and Indochina. Mahāyāna monks, for the most part, traveled with trade caravans along the Silk Road, carrying the dharma into Central Asia and China as early as the first century CE. So strongly identified with the Silk Road were the Mahāyāna missions that when the Chinese first encountered Buddhism they referred to it as the religion of the "foreign merchants." Its reception in China, as we will later see, was somewhat mixed, but owing to political conditions in China, and the persistence of Indian monks making pilgrimages there for several centuries, the soil was well prepared for the planting of this new faith.

It may seem that in this chapter we have moved somewhat far afield of the images we may automatically associate with Zen, but the purpose of providing this historical background will become clear as our narrative moves into China and Japan, where the Mahāyāna tradition flowered into new forms and transformed the histories of these civilizations. We must remember, again, that Zen, or *dhyāna*, has its roots in the Indian Buddhist tradition and was arguably *the* indispensable practice of Gautama himself. By the time Buddhism arrived in China, it was a full-blown religion complete with heavens, hells, saints, and deities; magic, medicine, rituals, and art; scriptures and theologies—supported by the force of a powerful empire and transmitted through the trading caravans of enterprising merchants. That such a constellation of effects began with one man sitting deep in meditation seeking an answer to the problem of the world's sufferings is a fact that we cannot forget or ignore.

3

THE CHAN SECT IN CHINA

In one of the more famous entries in the "official" collection of Zen puzzles known as *kōan*,[1] a monk asks the master Jōshu, "Why did Bodhidharma go from the west to the east?" Jōshu replies, "The oak tree in the garden," an answer that is *supposed* to suggest that there is no past, present, or future— meaning, perhaps, that the monk's question is seeking the wrong kind of information. As is the case with all *kōan*, the "answers" are not found through analysis or logical deduction but only through a flash of insight. Zen disciples have sought enlightenment by wrestling with such questions for nearly a thousand years.

However instructional the riddle of Bodhidharma's motives for traveling to China may be for the Zen monk, the question has its own uses for the historian, because careful consideration of the matter can only lead to one *rational* answer. The Bodhidharma obviously went from the west to the east to establish Zen! This mysterious monk, who came to China in the sixth century CE, was reckoned to be the twentieth-eighth patriarch of Indian Buddhism, numbered sequentially from Gautama himself. In the Zen tradition, he is honored as the first patriarch of the Chinese Chan sect and as such is recognized as the true progenitor of East Asian Zen.

Bodhidharma, was by no means the first Indian Buddhist to reach China. As we noted in chapter 2, pilgrims had been making the trek across Central Asia since the first century BCE and had settled in China since the first century CE, establishing temples and schools and teaching the dharma to the various tribes and communities they encountered. Kumarajiva (344–413 CE), the half-Indian and half-Kuchean (i.e., from Kucha, a kingdom in present-day western China) scholar who translated some of the foundational sutras from Sanskrit into Chinese, stands out not only as one of the great teachers of the era but as a living example of Buddhism's success as a missionary religion.

The dharma was generally well received by the Chinese, who found meaningful correspondences between the new doctrines and their own native philosophical traditions. The Zen scholar Heinrich Dumoulin even suggests that there existed an "inner kinship between ancient Chinese thought and Buddhism," which may have contributed to the lasting success of the Chinese missions.[2] It is worth taking a closer look at this kinship because by the time Buddhism had become the imperial religion in China during the Tang dynasty (618–907), and was being carried by Chinese missionaries throughout the East Asian world, it was declining almost to the point of extinction in its Indian homeland. If it were not for the transplanting of Zen from India to China, it is unlikely that it would have become the global cultural commodity we know today.

By any measure, the rise of Buddhism in China was an historical marvel. China had already given birth to two major philosophical traditions, Confucianism and Daoism, both of which were at least as old and venerable as Buddhism. Moreover, thanks to the patronage of Chinese emperors throughout the Han dynasty (206 BCE–220 CE), Confucianism was considered almost a state orthodoxy. This scope of this booklet does not permit a particularly detailed discussion of Confucianism or Daoism, but to the extent that each of these great philosophies may aid in our understanding of Zen, a few important points are worth noting. Because of its importance as the philosophical underpinning of almost all East Asian thought, perhaps we should begin with Confucianism.

The philosophy of Confucius (551–479 BCE) consists of ethical teachings that emphasize human relationships, social harmony, personal virtue, filial piety, and good governance. While Confucius regularly referred to the "Way of Heaven," his heaven was neither a celestial kingdom nor the dwelling place of a personal God who intervened in human affairs. The Way, or "Dao," as Confucius understood it, was similar to a spiritual template that ordered the proper functioning of the cosmos, including the state and human society. The aim of Confucian thought, as we read in the *Analects*, is the cultivation of virtue for the sake of forming intelligent and honest men capable of ruling the people with benevolence and sobriety. There is nothing "otherworldly" about it, which would suggest that a system like Buddhism, which seeks extinction from existence, the renunciation of desire, and final escape from rebirth, would not be viewed favorably by the scholar-officials of the Han government. Certainly the Confucians could admire the Buddhists' patriarchal devotion to the Buddha, which bore some resemblance to Confucian filial piety; the Mahāyāna preaching of compassion corresponded well enough to the Confucian notion of *ren* (humanity), and the Buddha himself, who after several centuries had acquired the trappings of something both human and divine, seemed to be a reasonable analog to the fabled Yellow Emperor of Chinese legend. For the most part, though, the essential transcendental and world-denying qualities of Buddhism did not sit well with the life-affirming and optimistic philosophy of Confucianism, nor did its yearning for detachment from human affairs resonate well with the relationship-driven complexity of Confucian social and political life. It seems to be no accident that the heyday of Buddhism took place only after the fall of the Han dynasty, when Confucian orthodoxy degenerated into the rampant corruption and violence that attended the empire's disintegration.

In the centuries of disunity following the Han, Buddhism came to play a political, as well as spiritual, role in China, as new contenders for political power adopted Buddhism as an organizing principle for their polities. Like Emperor Asoka in India, many of the up-and-coming rulers in post-Han China fashioned themselves as protectors of the dharma and appropriated the cosmic authority of the Buddha to define their own legitimacy. Arguably, then, to the extent that Confucianism posed certain philosophical obstacles to the spread of Buddhism, the decline of Confucianism removed these barriers, and Buddhism began to flourish after 200 CE.

The case of Daoism is more complex. This philosophy, considered by some to be China's indigenous religion, also looks to the Way of Heaven as its underlying absolute, although as an absolute, the Way of the Daoists is a remarkably relative thing. Daoism, a naturalistic worldview, values that which *is* rather than that which *ought to be*. According to Daoism, virtue cannot be "cultivated" by men. Virtue, as characterized in Laozi's *Dao Dejing*, is something ever present yet mysteriously hidden; it reveals itself when men avoid all forms of artifice and affectation and choose instead to follow their instincts. The models to emulate are not legendary heroes but the processes of nature itself. Daoists are urged, paradoxically, to be as still as mountains yet move as naturally as flowing water, to seek low places, as water does, and to strive for emptiness, uselessness, and simplicity. Rather than trying to order the world in the Confucian way, the Daoist prefers "nondoing," or *wu-wei*, believing that the real underlying order or nature will only emerge if things are left alone. Instead of displaying the superior attainments of the Confucian gentleman, the Daoist sage presents the appearance of an uncultivated rustic, perfectly in tune with nature and laughing at the contrived virtue of the scholar-official.

Based on what we already know about the Middle Way of the Buddha, we can see how Daoism would provide Buddhism a much more receptive ground than Confucianism did. While Daoists may have had difficulty with the idea of seeking extinction from life (many Daoists in their love for life ardently sought immortality), most of the tenets of Buddhism were perfectly agreeable to them—and Daoism was, by its own definition, open, receptive, and yielding. It is not fatuous to suggest—in fact several modern Zen scholars have explicitly argued it—that the historical fusion of Daoism and Mahāyāna Buddhism simply *is* Zen. In his *The Way of Zen*, the well-known popularizer of Zen in the West, Alan Watts, asserted that "the origins of Zen are as much Taoist [*sic*] as Buddhist."[3] Because many westerners who study Zen are also exposed to Daoism, there has been a tendency in the popular literature

to almost equate the two. To make such an equation may satisfy the desire in some Western seekers to lump various forms of "oriental wisdom" together, but it is historically inaccurate and does injury to the philosophical complexity of both Daoism and Zen Buddhism. We can say, though, that Chinese conditions, and to a considerable extent Daoism, did much to shape the development of Zen, and it is without question that the development of Mahāyāna in China unfolds almost inevitably toward the dominance of the Chan school.

According to tradition, Bodhidharma came to China in the sixth century, possibly in 520 CE, the year in which he apparently had an interview with Emperor Wu of the Liang

Figure 3.1. The First Chan Patriarch, Bodhidharma. This Japanese scroll calligraphy of Bodhidharma reads "Zen points directly to the human heart, see into your nature and become Buddha." It was created by Hakuin Ekaku (1685 to 1768).

state in north central China. The emperor, after boasting to Bodhidharma about the many temples he had built, the many sutras he had had translated, and the monasteries he had funded, asked how much merit he had gained from these good works. Bodhidharma's response, characteristic of his reputation as a blunt eccentric with little regard for earthly authority, was that these projects had brought him no merit at all. When the confused emperor asked him to explain what the basic teaching of the Buddha was, the monk replied, "Vast emptiness, and there is nothing in it to be called holy, sire!" When the emperor then asked him who he was, he answered, "I know not, sire!"[4] Modern students of Zen have seen in this exchange an early example of the Zen *mondo*, a question-and-answer session between the student and master that is more often than not highly frustrating for the student. The common perception we have today of idiosyncratic Zen masters insulting or belittling their students may have its prototype in Bodhidharma's brusque personal manner. After his audience with the emperor, Bodhidharma is said to have gone to a cave near the Shaolin monastery, where he spent nine years in meditation staring at the inner wall.[5] The primacy of "wall gazing," (*pi-kuan* in Chinese) appears in the treatise *Two Entrances and Four Acts*, a text attributed to Bodhidharma that claims there are two ways to enter the path to enlightenment. The first of these ways—"principle"—is based on knowledge of scripture, which leads, through intense "wall gazing," beyond words, texts, and forms into silent communion with all entities. Thus true knowledge is the awareness of nonduality, meaning that there is no "other" and no self distinct from the rest of the world, physical or mental. The second way—"practice"—entails four supplemental acts: (1) overturning hatred; (2) obeying karma; (3) silencing craving; and (4) being in tune with the dharma. If we consider these two entrances in the most concrete terms possible, we can conclude that the way to enlightenment is to embrace silence, to move beyond words and drop all forms of self-fixation. With the Bodhidharma's own practice, we can locate the origins of the Zen tradition: the privileging of meditation, the profession of nonduality, and pursuit of the mind-shattering flash of enlightenment that follows complete detachment from forms and expectations.

Bodhidharma did not establish any monastic communities in China, but he did acquire a good many disciples, the most illustrious of which was Huike (487–593 CE). The figure of a great many legends himself, Huike apparently entered into Bodhidharma's discipleship after waiting for many days in the snow outside the master's cave and being told repeatedly to go away because he was not ready for instruction. In an effort to prove his worthiness, Huike chopped off his arm and brought the bloody stump to Bodhidharma; this was sufficient to attract the attention of the wall-gazing master, who asked him what he wanted. "Please pacify my mind" said Huike. "Bring out your mind here before me and I will pacify it" said Bodhidharma. "But when I seek my own mind, I cannot find it," answered Huike. "There! I have pacified your mind!" shouted Bodhidharma. With this, Huike attained awakening.[6]

Here, again, we see the kinds of interchanges (complete with a radical act of physical violence!) that would come to exemplify the idiosyncratic relationships between masters and pupils in the Zen tradition. In varied ways, Bodhidharma's eccentricities stamped Zen with a reputation for wildness and unpredictability. Years later, as the Bodhidharma was nearing death, he gathered his closest disciples and asked them what each had attained. After each disciple sagely revealed the attainments of his own insight and enlightenment, Huike remained silent. Bodhidharma considered this the best answer and made Huike his successor, giving him his robe, his begging bowl, and four scrolls containing the *Lankāvatāra Sutra* (*The Sutra of Entering into Lanka*). Huike affirmed and propagated his master's teaching, the essentials of which are contained in the *Lankāvatāra*, an old Buddhist text, which teaches the primacy of the unitary mind over "identities" or "essences." As this sutra teaches, when one realizes that all the concrete and abstract entities of reality are merely pieces of one unified mind, one is able to see past the distinctions of false duality, and constructed otherness. At each step of the Zen propagation after Bodhidharma, we see the reinforcement of the notion that one must break away from phenomena in order to see past the illusory nature of distinctions.

The third Chan patriarch is thought to have been Sengcan (d. 606?), about whom very few historical details exist but to whom is usually attributed a text called *Xin Xin Ming*, or *On Believing in Mind*. This text affirms the teaching of nonduality, and oneness inside the mind.

> One in All, All in One—
> If only this is realized,
> No more worry about your not being perfect.[7]

Daoxin (580–651), the fourth patriarch, changed the trajectory of Chan by founding the first monastic community in Shuanfeng. From Daoxin forward, Chan would no longer be a sect of wandering mendicants but a community of monks concerned with the spiritualization of everyday work such as chopping wood and carrying water. Daoxin seems to have been a strong, responsible abbot who gathered a great many disciples and embodied the Chan way, spending long hours in *zazen* (sitting meditation) and warning his disciples to avoid useless conversation or any activities that would detract from the primary practice of meditation.

Hongren (601–74), the fifth patriarch, not only preserved the practices and doctrines of his predecessors but presided over a community that came to number nearly five hundred monks. In these early years of the Tang dynasty, Buddhism became a great cultural influence, not only in China but in the broader East Asian region, including Korea and Japan. Chan was the largest and arguably most important sect in China, and as abbot of the Dongshan (East Mountain) monastery, Hongren exercised a great deal of influence over the development of Tang Chinese culture. Unfortunately, Hongren also witnessed, and if the popular legends are true may have helped create, a split that would divide the Chan community along personal, geographical, and doctrinal lines. The origin of the dispute, according to legend, lies with the so-called *gatha* contest, in which Hongren, seeking to identify a worthy successor, asked his chief disciples to write a *gatha*, a religious verse, to prove their level of enlightenment. The heir apparent, at least according to his reputation in the monastery, was a monk named Shenxui, who wrote the following *gatha*.

> The body is the Bodhi tree (enlightenment),
> The mind is like a clear mirror standing
> Take care to wipe it all the time,
> Allow no grain of dust to cling

The verse was made public, much to the approval of the monks, none of whom doubted that Shenxui would receive the seal of transmission. Then, to the surprise of the entire community, an illiterate novice name Huineng (638–713), who had been assigned to various menial labors in the kitchen and on the monastery grounds, had his own *gatha* transcribed and presented to the community. Huineng's verse read as follows.

> The Bodhi is not like a tree
> The clear mirror is nowhere standing
> Fundamentally not one thing exists;
> Where, then, is the grain of dust to cling?[8]

This verse, exhibiting a deeper understanding of nonduality and nondiscrimination, was judged by Hongren to be superior. Hongren named the young kitchen servant his successor and ordered him to flee the monastery lest he suffer the jealous wrath of Shenxui and his supporters. Huineng escaped at night across the Jiang (Yangzi) River and established what is known to Zen historians as the "southern sect" of the Chan school. This particular legend, obviously, is part of the lore of the southern sect, which emerged triumphant against its northern rival and depicts Huineng as possessing superior dharma and bravery compared to those of Shenxui and his faction. The truth behind the split may not be quite so dramatic, as other stories indicate that Shenxui and Huineng respected one another throughout their lives. It is true, though, that the northern and southern sects, as we know them, had different views about the means of attaining enlightenment, and there is no doubt that great animosity grew between the successors of Hongren's two great disciples.

The arguments between the two schools in later generations were not just political (i.e., rival claims over the patriarchate) but also doctrinal. The southern school accused the northern school of teaching a false path to enlightenment, one that was too bound to material reality, too concerned with method, and too concerned with making distinctions between things. As evidenced, perhaps, in Shenxui's *gatha*, the northern school was too concerned about the "mirror" and the "dust" that might cling to it. The southern sect, following the spirit of Huineng, maintained that true Chan looked past the standing mirror and the clinging dust and instead evoked the primacy of "nothingness" in which ultimate reality could be found. In practical terms, the northern sect could be considered a school of "gradual" enlightenment whose adherents believed that passions and desires could be overcome through sustained discipline and meditation. Adherents of the southern school, on the other hand, believed in the possibility of "sudden" enlightenment and felt that discipline and study were secondary. True enlightenment came with a flash, as the Buddha's had come, with the awareness that all things are One. Getting bogged down in terms, definitions, signs, and sutras was potentially misleading.

Breaking the Bodhidharma's "Twofold Path" into antagonistic theories of awakening created an unfortunate rift in the Chan community. As many Zen scholars have observed, it was probably a false distinction from the start. Enlightenment rarely came to anybody "in a flash"; the flash of insight almost always came only after years of preparation and mental discipline. The Buddha's Eightfold Path was a method of life, not a formula for instant success. The observant Western student might find it odd that a community of monks so obsessed with seeing beyond duality would have broken into factions. For Chan Buddhists to cling to such a duality seems ironic to say the least. Nevertheless, disputes of this kind have continued in the Zen school into the present day.

Huineng's southern sect prevailed over the northern sect, which soon disappeared, and his doctrine of no-mind, which brought the seeker into complete and sudden detachment from all phenomena, mental or material, remained the core principle of Chan during its golden age in China. Although Huineng was the last recognized "patriarch" of the Chan sect, his doctrine was preserved in the teachings of the so-called Five Schools of Guiyang,

Yunmen, Fayan, Linji, and Caodong. The first three of these schools, founded by disciples of Huineng, also dwindled, although the last two, Linji and Caodong, perhaps known better by their Japanese names Rinzai and Sōtō, became dominant and have remained so into the present day. I will discuss the growth and doctrines of these two important schools in chapter 5, but for now it might be worthwhile to take stock and see what the emergence of Chan in China contributes to our narrative of Zen.

Chinese Chan Buddhism represents far more than historical connective tissue between Indian Buddhism and Japanese Zen. It marks the spot where the *dhyāna* tradition became distinctively East Asian and the Mahāyāna school developed the doctrines, monastic forms, and interpretive lore that have earned Zen a unique place among world religious traditions. In this, Buddhism proved its ability to adapt to a variety of cultural contexts, and the meditative practices of ancient India proved their own universal applicability, becoming the property of an integrated world spirituality. In the next chapter, we will take a brief detour to look at some of the doctrines and sutras in greater depth, as well as some of the remarkable figures who taught and practiced them.

4

THE SCRIPTURAL ORIGINS
OF EMPTINESS

U p to this point we have traced the historical origins of Buddhism, the migration of the Mahāyāna teaching into China, and the development of the Chan sect in China from the time of its founder, Bodhidharma, up through that of the sixth patriarch, Huineng. We have also briefly considered several key concepts of Chan Buddhism, not only the indispensable practice of sitting meditation, or *zazen*, but also core ideas such as nonduality, detachment, and "one mind." Hopefully, this chapter will solidify our understanding of some of these ideas by looking a little more deeply at *their* histories, including the traditions and texts in which they unfold.

Like all sects of the Mahāyāna school, the teachings of Zen are rooted in the doctrine of *prajñāpāramitā*, "the perfection of wisdom." *Prajñāpāramitā* refers specifically to the transcendental state of consciousness reached by the Buddha during his enlightenment on earth. A series of texts known as the *prajñāpāramitā* sutras, the earliest of which date to the first century BCE, were believed by their devotees to amplify the teachings of the Buddha on a metaphysical level far beyond the original meanings set forth by the elders. The authors of these texts were not trying to overturn the "orthodox" teachings of the elders; rather, they wanted to emphasize what they believed were the essential truths of the Buddha's experience. What, then, *were* the essential truths of this experience?

We remember that in the third Noble Truth the Buddha proclaimed that the key to the cessation of suffering was to bring an end to "desire," by which he meant the attachment to worldly things and ideas. The *prajñāpāramitā* sutras open the way to nonattachment by declaring that the things and ideas (or entities, dharmas) of the phenomenal world are illusory, devoid of any substance—in a word, empty.[1] Attaining clear awareness of this emptiness, expressed in the term *sunyata* and often translated as the "void," is the "goal" of the person following the Buddhist path. On entering the void, the disciple realizes that even the thinking self is devoid of substance and sees that there is no self that really does any thinking. In other words, there is no distinction between the self and any object of thought, or even between the self and the process of thinking. This breakthrough takes the disciple into a place beyond thought, beyond the need to hold on to any idea of separation from any other thing, and represents the awakening (*samadhi*) to "suchness" (*tathata*) that leads to freedom from attachment. With his or her awakening, the disciple comes into possession of complete enlightenment inside the all-knowing mind of the Buddha. The importance of *sunyata*, then, is that it annihilates the false constructs of the mind, including the illusion of duality, and reveals the "suchness" behind things, bringing full consciousness, or "all-knowing," as a result.

To illustrate the idea concretely, consider what is probably the most important of these scriptures, and surely the most accessible: a short sutra called the *Heart of the Prajñāpāramitā*. Known more commonly as the *Heart Sutra*, this text contains the essential precepts of the doctrine of "perfected wisdom." The *Heart Sutra* opens with the bodhisattva Avalokitesvara meditating on the five "*skhandas*,"[2] a Sanskrit term that Zen scholar D. T. Suzuki translates as "elements" or "aggregates," the constituents of human activity and form.[3] The first aggregate is physical form, the second is sensation, the third is thinking, the fourth is will, and the fifth is consciousness. Avalokitesvara declares that they are all empty and tells his disciple Sariputra of his realization.

> "O Sariputra, form here is emptiness, emptiness is form; form is no other than emptiness, emptiness is no other than form. . . . all things are characterized with emptiness; they are not born, they are not annihilated; they are not tainted, they are not immaculate, they do not increase, they do not decrease."[4]

Since the aggregates are empty, there is no way anybody could possess accurate knowledge of anything based on sensation or thought—needless to say, this includes almost all of the knowledge that people generally consider to be real. Avalokitesvara concludes that only a mind free of attachment from these aggregates can dwell in perfected wisdom and attain nirvana. The last verse of the *Heart Sutra* is one of the most famous passages in all of Buddhist literature.

> "*Gate, gate, paragate, parasamgate, bodhi svaha*"—"O Bodhi [wisdom], gone, gone, gone to the other shore, landed at the other shore."[5]

This *gatha*, like the *kōan* that alludes to the folly of continuing to carry one's raft after one has crossed a stream, suggests that the truly enlightened disciple, having crossed over to wisdom no longer needs to rely on the five aggregates.

The *Heart Sutra* and the rest of *prajñāpāramitā* were not part of the Theravada school's canon, and so they occupied only a peripheral place in the early monastic community. Thanks to the efforts of the Indian scholar-monk Nagarjuna, who lived between 150 and 250 CE, these scriptures enjoyed a revival in the second century CE and became something of a supplementary canon on which the Mahāyāna tradition was built. Nagarjuna's careful study of these texts, as well as his own writings on nonduality and emptiness, led to a formalization of the precepts of "perfected wisdom." The "logic" of *prajñāpāramitā*, which Nagarjuna presents as a kind of interplay between "being" and "nonbeing," was learned and transmitted by a fervent group of Indian monks, many of whom became the missionary pilgrims to Central Asia and China. As we saw in the case of Bodhidharma, these monks brought more than just a doctrine of transcendence but also a method of stilling the mind to attain its fruits. That method was *dhyāna*, the sitting meditation.

It should come as no surprise that the Chan masters bore a special devotion to the *prajñāpāramitā* sutras. As discussed in chapter 3, Bodhidharma was said to have given his beloved scrolls of the *Lankāvatāra Sutra* to Huike as part of the accoutrements of patriarchal office, telling him that with this sutra he would be able to save the whole world. The *Lankāvatāra's* teaching of nonsubstantiality is among the more radical expressions of perfected wisdom, claiming that all the phenomena of the world are merely creations of the mind or figments of mental energy. In this long, complex, and multilayered text, the Buddha appears at the Castle of Lanka (in Sri Lanka) and begins to preach to a great assembly of monks about the perfection of wisdom. In a long series of often confusing discourses and discussions, he reveals to Mahamati, a spokesman for the assembly, that although the things of the world are no more substantial than dreams, imaginings, or memories, people remain trapped in them out of ignorance and ego attachment.

> The Blessed One said this to him: Mahamati, since the ignorant and simple-minded, not knowing that the world is what is seen of Mind itself, cling to the multitudinousness of external objects, cling to the notions of being and non-being, oneness and otherness, bothness, and non-bothness, existence and non-existence, eternity and non-eternity, and having the character of self-substance, which idea rises from discrimination based on habit-energy, they are addicted to false imaginings.[6]

The way to break free of the entrapments of these "false imaginings" is to recognize one's attachment to existence and, through practice of the correct *dhyāna* (meditation), learn to discard appearances and images and come into attunement with the suchness of the Buddha mind.

[W]hen the existence and non-existence of the external world are understood to be due to the seeing of the Mind itself in these signs [appearances], the Bodhisattva can enter upon the stage of imagelessness where Mind-only is, and there see into the Solitude which underlies the discrimination of all things as being and non-being, and the deep-seated attachments resulting therefrom.[7]

In addition to its reinforcing the notion that enlightenment comes from the realization of emptiness, the *Lankāvatāra Sutra* also speaks of a nonlinear "womb of suchness" in which awakening takes place as a kind of "revulsion." Suzuki interprets this revulsion as a "revolutionary" self-realization, implying the "suddenness" of awakening that became the ideal of the southern Chan school of Huineng and his disciples.

[T]hose who, afraid of sufferings arising from the discrimination of birth and death, seek for Nirvana, do not know that birth and death and Nirvana are not to be separated the one from the other; and seeing that all things subject to discrimination have no reality imagine that Nirvana consists in the further annihilation of the senses and their fields. They are not aware . . . of the fact that Nirvana is the all-conserving consciousness where a revulsion takes place by self-realization.[8]

Because the *Lankāvatāra Sutra* is one of the more obscure texts in the *prajñāpāramitā* tradition, D. T. Suzuki recommends reading it and meditating on it only in small pieces. We can imagine even Bodhidharma, whose powers of meditation were prodigious, doing likewise. We remember that his "Twofold Entrance" to the path spoke of using a passage of scripture as a kind of springboard for meditation, assuring his disciples that it would take them beyond words and meanings. Anybody looking for a logical, organized argument in any of the *prajñāpāramitā* sutras will be frustrated. Clearly their purpose was not to be "read" as a narrative but to be meditated on and ideally experienced as perfected wisdom.

One sutra that is easily read in its entirety—it is still regularly chanted in less than an hour in Zen temples—is the "Illusion-Cutting Diamond," commonly known as the *Diamond Sutra*. It is said that the patriarch Huineng attained enlightenment from hearing only a fragment of this sutra, which confirms the text's own claim that if only four lines were preserved for posterity, their recitation would result in immeasurable delight for whoever heard it. The sutra takes the form of a conversation between the Buddha and an elder, Subhuti, in which the Buddha attempts to clarify for Subhuti the true nature of mind and phenomena. What is revealed and reinforced in this dynamic question-and-answer session is that any held perception about reality is ultimately inauthentic because all perceptions are illusions. The famous last four lines of this sutra sum up its message succinctly.

All composite things
Are a like a dream, a phantasm, a bubble, and a shadow,
They are thus to be regarded.[9]

The early Chinese Chan authors completely incorporated the essence of Indian *prajñāpāramitā* in their own sermons and scriptures. In addition to Bodhidharma's original Twofold Entrance, we can point to numerous examples that show us that the "aim of the Chan Buddhist [was] the same as that of the *prajñāpāramitā* philosopher."[10] The *Transmission of the Lamp*, a collection of the lives and acts of the Chinese Chan masters compiled during the Song dynasty (960–1279) discloses the depth of the understanding and devotion that the Chan masters exhibited toward perfected wisdom. For example, we have the fourth patriarch and first great abbot, Daoxin, expounding to his student Fayung on the matter of nonbeing.

> All the hindrances to the attainment of *bodhi* (wisdom) which arise from passions that generate karma are originally non-existent. Every cause and effect is but a dream. There is not a triple world [the three realms of existence: desire, form, and formlessness] which one leaves and no *bodhi* to search for. The inner reality and outer appearance of man and ten thousand things are identical. The great Tao is formless and boundless. It is free from thought and anxiety.[11]

Fayung himself became a great dharma teacher, and, although he was formally attached to Daoxin's monastery, he found himself on occasion called to give lectures to public officials. Once when asked by a certain Prince Po-ling to comment on the cause of mental attitudes, he replied:

> When a mental attitude and the external word emerge, the natures of both are non-existent. Originally there is no knower of the cause of the emergence. The capacity of mind and the known are identical. When their origin is illumined, all that is in emergence no longer emerges. Emergence itself ceases.[12]

With each passing generation in Chinese Chan Buddhism, we can see both a deepening of devotion to the *prajñāpāramitā* and an increasing "nativization" of the tradition. The transplanting of Mahāyāna Buddhism was more than merely a migration from India to China; it was an appropriation, perhaps even a redefinition, of Mahāyāna into something fully Chinese. Perhaps the most interesting result of this change was the final transformation of a teaching that had been peripheral, if not heterodox, in India into something that was arguably the orthodoxy of Buddhism in China. As Chan developed between the sixth and ninth centuries, *prajñāpāramitā* became the new standard—and the new seedbed—of Buddhism throughout the East Asian region. The best illustration of this reality can be found in a text known as the *Platform Sutra*, which consists, for the most part, of a discourse on *prajñāpāramitā* given by the sixth Zen patriarch Huineng. This foundational sermon affirms the principles of nonbeing, sudden enlightenment, meditation, and nondualism yet places these principles squarely within the Chinese tradition through a recapitulation of the history of the Chan school since Bodhidharma. By the time of Huineng's patriarchate, Chan was a fully distinct and autonomous religious tradition.

Figure 4.1. The Sixth Zen Patriarch Huineng Cutting Bamboo. Liang Kai, Southern Song Dynasty, 13th century.

The purpose of this chapter has not been to give an exhaustive account of the *prajñāpāramitā* sutras or the early Chinese texts but to bring the doctrinal examination somewhat up to speed with the historical narrative. Now that we have circled back on Huineng, we can note again that with the sixth and last patriarch we see the completion of the transformation of Indian Mahāyāna Buddhism into Chinese Chan Buddhism, a transformation that marks both a fulfillment of Mahāyāna and the birth of Zen. As the Zen popularizer Alan Watts observed, even though there may not have been a formal *dhyāna* school in India, the meditative spirit of *prajñāpāramitā* was arguably recast as the essence of Chan, a possibility that invites us to consider some very big questions. First, can the doctrine of perfected wisdom be considered a "universal" religious value or is it merely an exported native tradition? If it is an export, how can it have been so richly possessed by two such different cultures as those of China and India? Another question along these lines is the consideration of whether or not *prajñāpāramitā* is *true*. If we throw all cultural trappings aside, and look at Chan from the ethical standpoint, does the possibility that all reality is empty require us to think and live in a different way? A good Zen Buddhist would probably conclude that these questions ultimately have no meaning, but they are certainly worth pondering as we prepare to encounter yet another major transplanting of the dharma—this time from China to Japan.

5

ZEN COMES TO JAPAN

The arrival of Buddhism in Japan is customarily dated to 552 CE, the year Emperor Kimmei received a statue of the Buddha and a collection of sutras as a gift from a delegation of Korean monks. The Chinese missions in East Asia were a natural outgrowth of the Tang dynasty's exuberant cultural expansion, and throughout the period waves of colonizing monks carried the doctrines, practices, and artifacts of Chinese Buddhism into Japan, initially through the activities of Korean missionaries. The most successful missions were carried out by the Tiantai (in Japanese, Tendai), Zhenyan (in Japanese, Shingon), and Huayen (in Japanese, Kegon) sects of the Mahāyāna school; the representation of the Chan sect was all but nonexistent. It would take more than six hundred years for a certified Zen master to create a permanent establishment in Japan, which means that when it did finally make its appearance, the Zen sect was still very Chinese in its expression and was looked on as something of an alien religion by some of the more established and nativized monastic Buddhist communities. The planting, growth, and flowering of Zen constitute one of the most remarkable explosions of cross-cultural fertilization the world has ever seen—so much so that Zen, despite its rich Indian and Chinese antecedents, has become, particularly among foreigners, all but synonymous with Japanese culture.[1]

The tendency of many contemporary westerners to "equate" Zen to Japan may stem from interpretations of the works of D.T. Suzuki (1870–1966), a twentieth-century Japanese scholar who spent his life trying to communicate the complexities of Zen to foreign students. We will take up Suzuki's "project" in more detail in the next chapter, but for now we should note that he spent over sixty years producing translations of Zen texts, largely with the purpose of making Zen—and Japan—understandable to the English-speaking world. It is not surprising that many of his readers would come to identify Zen as the essential feature of *all* Japanese cultural forms. Suzuki, though thoroughly schooled in the history of Buddhism, was content to let this misconception linger. Not only did he feel that Zen could assist in Japan's rehabilitation after World War II, but he also sincerely believed that Japanese Zen holds a unique place among the various sects of historical Buddhism. As we will see in chapter 7, Zen contributed a great deal to the formation of the early Japanese national identity, so we can, perhaps, understand why a modern Japanese scholar would deliberately seek to conflate Zen and Japanese culture. That being said, we need to be wary of perpetuating less than perfect associations and take a more objective look at the relationship between Japan and Zen Buddhism.

In this chapter we will examine the early history of Japanese Zen, focusing on historical and doctrinal developments that took place during the Kamakura period (1185–1333), when Zen first began to flourish in Japan.

The Kamakura was a period of revolutionary transition in Japanese history, a time of vigorous new beginnings that fatefully coincided with a prolonged period of crisis in China, namely, the collapse of the Song dynasty (960–1279), and the subsequent Mongol regime, which ruled in China between 1279 and 1368. For much of its premodern history, Japan's development was linked, at least indirectly, to the political fortunes of imperial China. During periods in which the Chinese empires were strong, Japan's status often tended toward a tributary relationship with the "Middle Kingdom." During periods of crisis that undermined China's ability to manage its diplomatic periphery, the influence of Chinese culture receded and Japan's rulers used their relative autonomy to concentrate on cultivating native institutions. In light of this dynamic, the Song dynasty was unusual in that even in its strongest days it was not aggressively expansionist but rather focused on the economic benefits of trade with Japan. Song rulers were regularly beset with military and diplomatic crises, culminating in their capitulation to their former Mongol "allies" who systematically conquered southern China between 1259 and 1279.

For most of the Song dynasty, Japan engaged in peaceful trade with the Chinese and developed what many historians consider to be one of the most glorious cultural epochs in the history of civilization. This was the classical Heian period (794–1185) in which Japanese political life was largely defined by an aesthetic culture that produced a profusion of written works—mostly authored by aristocratic women—that continue to rank among the masterpieces of world literature. Romances such as the *Tale of Genji*, diaries such as the *Sarashina Nikki*, and random journals such as the *Pillow Book of Sei Shonagon* recorded the courtly elegance and aesthetic refinement of an intensely self-absorbed aristocratic minority, led by the imperial regents of the Fujiwara family. In all of this literature, we find evidence of the long-acculturated Buddhism of Japan's aristocracy, in particular an emphasis on the idea of impermanence and the cult of beauty, which stemmed from the contemplation of passing things. The Buddhist communities of Heian Japan enjoyed their own moment of splendor, growing in wealth and influence under the direction of wellborn abbots and sharing the aesthetic ideals of the political elites. The monasteries grew so powerful from their landholdings that it was often unclear whether the abbots' primary concern was estate management or the perfection of dharma. Eventually, the Heian polity began to sag under the weight of its own imbalanced priorities. In the countryside, where a class of rusticated nobles took charge of the economy—while the rulers held poetry contests—opportunism took the place of good stewardship. In the capital, the allure of court entertainments and palace intrigue took precedence over statecraft. As the priorities of the imperial household shifted from administration to patronage brokering, ambitious regents and "retired" emperors began to exercise an increasing degree of unofficial power over the throne.

In 1156, an imperial succession dispute led to a civil disturbance in which both camps enlisted the help of rural warrior clans to help them press their claims. The real outcome of the struggle was the destruction of the old Heian aristocracy as a new order of warrior elites took control of the capital and the government. In successive conflicts in 1159 and 1180, the Minamoto and Taira military families fought for control of the country, with the victory ultimately going to Minamoto no Yoritomo, who became the first shogun, or military governor, in Japanese history. Yoritomo's in-laws in the Hōjō clan would rule Japan for over a century—granting their patronage to the Zen school, which, like their own regime, represented a dynamic departure from the stagnation and corruption of the old ways.

For many Japanese living through this turbulent and dangerous transition, the collapse of the Heian civilization was felt to be an historical rupture on the order of world-ending catastrophe. According to some interpretations of Buddhist eschatology—the study of "end-times"—the world had entered its final historical age, or "*mappō*," in the year 1052. Because *mappō* was believed to be an age of such degenerate dharma that people would be powerless to save themselves, the period witnessed several new sects that stressed simple faith in the power of the Buddha to save all sentient beings. By salvation, the priests of the new sects did not mean "awakening," and they did not see the Buddha as an exemplar of the "middle way," but rather as a divine savior who descended from paradise to escort the souls of the faithful into the "Pure Land" upon death. Among these sects were the Pure Land Sect and the True Pure Land Sect—both of which urged a simple faith in the name of the Amida Buddha. The Lotus Sect, founded by the firebrand Nichren, was another popular sect that called on believers simply to chant the name of the *Lotus Sutra* in order to gain merit for themselves and their troubled country.

Zen entered this colorful milieu of popular worship as a no-nonsense sect that cared little for whether or not the world was ending and had no particular interest in personal saviors descending from heaven on purple clouds. When the master Eisai, newly home from China, established the Shōfukuji meditation hall in Hakata in 1191 he was met with hostility by monks of the established Tendai sect. Fortunately for the fate of Zen in Japan, Eisai won the favor of the shogun with the promulgation of *The Spread of Zen for the Protection of the Country*. By gaining the official backing of the *bakufu*, the warrior government in Kamakura, which authorized the construction of several new Zen temples, Eisai gave life to both the monastic and the military caste associations that have distinctly shaped Zen's history in Japan.

The long, mutually fruitful, and often controversial association between Zen and the Japanese military can be explained in part by the fact that Zen, which values austerity and self-discipline and makes no substantial distinction between life and death, offered an inherent spiritual attraction for a class of men whose lives were constantly on the line. While the great majority of Japanese soldiers were not practicing Zen Buddhists, many of the samurai ruling elites embraced the discipline and philosophy of Zen and left the distinctive stamp of their tastes and values on it. The fusion of military and Zen culture in Kamakura Japan, and more so in the following Muromachi period (1333–1573), only proved the adaptability of a religious tradition that had already been substantially transformed by the influences of an external political culture.

To be sure, Zen had undergone remarkable outward changes between the time of the passing of the sixth patriarch Huineng in 713 and Eisai's first temple in Japan. Chan, which we know had once been divided into the northern and southern schools, became even further divided into five subsidiary schools, each led by one of Huineng's disciples. After several generations, only two of these schools, Linchi (in Japanese, Rinzai) and Caodong (in Japanese, Sōtō), remained. These two streams, which remain the dominant schools of Zen even today, were already established when Chinese Buddhism suffered an irreversible setback in 845. This was the year the Daoist emperor Wuzong (814–46) declared war on the great Buddhist monasteries, using the rationale that their belief systems were unacceptably foreign and their tax-free status an excessive burden on the dwindling treasury of the Tang empire. Fortunately for the Chan sect, its ascetic and industrious monks were perceived as frugal enough to escape condemnation as imperial enemies; it may also be that their beliefs were traditionally close enough to Daoism to spare them Wuzong's wrath, which fell hard on such sects as the Tiantai and Huayen. While each of these other sects lived on in its respective Japanese branches, only the Chan survived in China, outlasting the Tang dynasty itself and flourishing in the subsequent short "Five Dynasties" period and the illustrious Song dynasty that followed.

The Chan monasteries greatly influenced the cultural "renaissance" of the Song dynasty, contributing not only to new styles in literature and ink painting but transforming intellectual life as well, as their study halls became discussion centers for the new political philosophy of neo-Confucianism. Perhaps the most important doctrinal development of Song dynasty Zen was the institutionalization of the customs of the Linchi and Caodong schools. While both schools honored the legacy of their common patriarch, Huineng, each placed different emphasis on the nature of attaining enlightenment. The Linchi sect, in general, adhered to its founder's valorization of sudden enlightenment, which could be precipitated by surprising and even violent acts. The Caodong sect endorsed a more gradual ascent to enlightenment through a series of stages or "ranks." This divergence recapitulates the older argument between the southern and northern schools. The fact that it reappeared as a new split between two branches of the prevailing southern ("sudden enlightenment") school shows that it was a thorny and persistent matter, not one easily or decisively resolved.

By the time Zen came to Japan, the question had been largely wrapped in the practical matters of means—so much so that according to common understanding, the chief difference between the schools is that the Rinzai favored seeking enlightenment through the means of "solving" *kōan*, which, again, are riddles that defy logical analysis, and the Sōtō sect, which favored the attainment of enlightenment through the gradual means of *zazen* or sitting meditation. To some degree this is accurate, but this dichotomy oversimplifies the critical matter of exactly *how* enlightenment is attained and exactly "what it looks like" when it is experienced. For the Rinzai monks, the essence of Zen is the instantaneous experience of awakening, and for Sōtō monks the essence of Zen is the practice of *zazen* itself. Historically the question is important because the implications of whether awakening is available to anybody at any time or only accessible to those who have made the right preparations determine the degree to which any particular culture may adapt to Zen and how readily that culture may reshape Zen. Some examples may clarify the difference in a more concrete way.

The "sudden enlightenment" stream of the Chinese Linji school has an illustrious, if quirky, history that reaches all the way back to the first disciples of Huineng. One of these was Mazu (707–86), a monk who scrupulously strove for enlightenment through intense meditation, only to achieve it suddenly after an embarrassment at the hands of his teacher. Observing Mazu in earnest meditation one day, the master asked him what he was trying to do. Mazu replied that he was trying to become a Buddha. At this point the master picked up a tile and began polishing it, and Mazu asked him why he was polishing the tile. The master replied that he was trying to make a mirror. When Mazu asked how he expected to make a mirror out of a tile by polishing it, the master replied by asking how Mazu expected to become a Buddha by sitting in meditation. At that moment the folly of his ambition became clear, and Mazu attained enlightenment. He became a legendary master himself, championing the technique of *katsu*, "the shout," as a means of helping monks break through the stagnation of their own meditation. This took the form of yelling at disciples, striking them, or committing some equally out of the ordinary act to jolt them out of their spiritual stagnation.

Another forerunner of the Linji school was Deshan (781–867), a monk who began as a northern school "gradualist" determined to challenge the doctrine of the southern school. He journeyed to the south, equipped with commentaries on the *Diamond Sutra* and fully prepared to do dharma battle with the southern monks. In the vicinity of the monastery, he met an old woman on the roadside and asked her for food and drink. She asked the young scholar what he was carrying in his pack, and learning that it was a text on the *Diamond Sutra*, she pointed out that according to the diamond cutter there was no "self" that needed food or drink. Taken aback by her response, he continued to the monastery where he met the master, Lungtan. Already rattled at having been bested by the old woman, he sat in meditation to still his mind. At the end of the session, the master offered him a candle to light his way from the meditation hall, but just as Deshan took it the master blew it out, leaving him in utter darkness. At this moment, Deshan attained the sudden enlightenment whose existence he had come south to dispute. The next day, he burned his texts, having determined that they were unnecessary for the attainment of awakening.

Linji himself (d. 866) may have experienced the most traumatic awakening on record. For years he had studiously tried to attain enlightenment, only to suffer failure, as well as the insults and slaps of his master, Huangpo. Finally, Linji pointedly asked Huangpo what the essence of the Buddha mind was, and in return he received twenty blows with a stick, which drove him from Huangpo's temple to take up instruction elsewhere. When Linji told his new master what abuses Huangpo had inflicted on him, the new master responded by telling him that Huangpo had actually shown him great kindness. On hearing this, Linji was awakened and broke through the emotional barrier that years of anxiety and an intense desire to please had thrown up in his path. After his enlightenment, he returned to Huangpo's temple and slapped him in the face, much to the satisfaction of his old teacher.

What we can see, then, is that for those who believe in "sudden enlightenment" there is no formula or text or practice for attaining enlightenment; one is as likely to attain awakening by being struck with a stick as by practicing sitting meditation for twenty years. This was the crux of the argument of the Linji school against the Caodong monks, whose five-stage ascent to enlightenment could only be achieved through *zazen*. So opposed were the Linji monks to the idea that *only* sitting and quiet could bring illumination that some accused the Caodong adherents of following a "false path."[2] Leaving matters of method aside, the Linji masters had little room in which to question the legitimacy of the Caodong school in terms of its lineage and pedigree. The Caodong founders Dongshan and Caoshan also belonged to a line of transmission reaching back to Huineng. Their antecedent was the illustrious Shitou, or "Stone-head," whose song *Cantongqi* (in Japanese, Sandokai), *The Identity of Relative and Absolute*, restates the *prajñāpāramitā* essentials of emptiness and nonduality and reinforces the dialectic of being and nonbeing in terms of relative and absolute qualities of phenomena.

> To be attached to things is illusion
> To encounter the absolute is not yet enlightenment
> Each and all the subjective and objective spheres are related, and at the
>   same independent.
> Related and yet working differently.[3]

Shitou's insight into the coincidence of the relative and the absolute led to the Caodong school's articulation of degrees of combination between the two; these degrees became equivalent to grades of advancement from the pure relative to the pure absolute and were treated as something like milestones along the path to the realization that all relative phenomena exist in absolute union. Since interior stillness aided the relative mind in coming to awareness of its own absolute identity, it should only follow that this school would value centering through meditation over the unpredictable and often violent activity that could be implied by the possibility of sudden enlightenment.

It would be wrong to suppose that the differences in emphasis between sudden and gradual enlightenment were the cause of deep animosity or sectarian conflict. As we see in Japan during the Kamakura period, both schools used *kōan* as a means of training the mind, and both schools practice *zazen* as the primary meditative practice in the monastic setting. The difference is really more a difference in preference or emphasis, not unlike the differences between Dominicans and Franciscans within the Roman Catholic tradition. It seems clear from history that people of different temperaments were drawn to the different schools—the Rinzai, perhaps, appealing to the active life and the Sōtō to the contemplative. In the Japanese tradition, each school can point to an especially gifted and dynamic Kamakura period founder; for the Rinzai, it was Eisai, mentioned earlier, and for the Sōtō, it was Dōgen, one of the greatest thinkers in Japanese history.

The elder of the two, Eisai (1141–1215), began his religious training in childhood as a novice in the Tendai sect and made a study trip to China in his youth. While there, he became interested in the Chan teachings and came to believe that the disciplines of the Rinzai school would do much to sharpen the laxity of monastic life as he had seen it in the Tendai temples of Kyoto. He returned to Japan in 1191, bringing the Zen dharma and a packet of green tea seeds with him. He planted both in Hakata on Japan's southwestern coast, establishing, as I have noted, the Shōfukuji temple, the first permanent Zen community in Japan.

Despite the initial opposition of the Tendai establishment, the Rinzai school enjoyed vigorous growth in its early years. Eisai personally oversaw the establishment of several monasteries, Kenninji (1202), in the cultural capital of Kyoto, and Jufukuji (1200), in the political capital of Kamakura. All of the Rinzai temples enjoyed the patronage of the Hōjō ruling clan, but the two named here attained special status, being ranked among the "Five Mountains" in their respective locations. The designation Five Mountains was carried over from the Chan school in China and referred to temples that were both supported and regulated by the state. The first Chinese temples had actually been built on mountains, but by the time the name was adopted in Japan *mountain* stood for the temple itself, and was symbolic of the prominence of the temple, in the eyes of both the Zen community and the *bakufu*.

Each temple was laid out in a similar fashion, beginning with the "mountain gate," a physical and spiritual barrier that often contained images of the *arhats*—sixteen enlightened saints of Indian Buddhism. The gate led into the temple grounds, on which could be found the large *butsuden*, or Buddha hall, which served as the main ceremonial building. There were also a storehouse for temple relics, the abbot's quarters, bathhouses, and the dharma hall—a small auditorium for formal lectures on doctrine. Arguably, the most important building was the meditation hall, where the monks practiced *zazen* night and day, tirelessly working out the *kōan* that their abbots had chosen for them.

The *kōan* themselves were not just randomly picked. As discussed in chapter 3, there had existed since the Song dynasty two major collections of *kōan*, complete with "solutions" and commentaries by illustrious teachers. These compilations—the *Blue Cliff Record* (1125) and *Mumonkan* or *Gateless Gate* (1228)—contained the odd stories and paradoxical episodes that had become lore in the Zen tradition and were believed to be efficacious in bringing a monk to the state of awakening. The purpose behind the *kōan*, as we have also seen, was not to encourage a rational, logical solution to the situation proposed but to force the mind *out* of the box of reason and logic and into a state of crisis by forcing it to grasp with irrationality—with the expectation that when the mind came to an impasse, it would experience a breakthrough leading to awakening. What kind of paradox might be capable of bringing about such a radical flash of illumination? Below are several examples that reflect the idiosyncratic worldview of the Rinzai school.[4]

Nan Ch'uan Kills a Cat

At Nan Ch'uan's place one day the monks of the eastern and western halls were arguing about a cat. When Nan Ch'uan saw this, he then held up the cat and said, "If you can speak then I will not kill it." No one in the community replied. Nan Ch'uan cut the cat into two pieces. (*Blue Cliff Record*, case 63)

A monk asked Pai Chang, "What's the extraordinary affair?" Chang said, "Sitting alone on Ta Hsiung Mountain." The monk bowed, Chang thereupon hit him. (*Blue Cliff Record*, case 26)

A monk asked Master Tozan, "What is Buddha?" Tozan said, "Three pounds of flax." (*Mumonkan*, case 18)

Goso said, "To give an example, it is like a buffalo passing through a window. Its head, horns, and four legs have all passed through. Why is it that its tail cannot?" (*Mumonkan*, case 38)

Whether or not a disciple had actually *attained* awakening through meditation was determined by the master, who in a face-to-face ritual known as *sanzen* would judge the fruits of the student's meditation. It usually took years for a monk to attain enlightenment from working through a *kōan*, which suggests that even in Rinzai Zen there was nothing necessarily "sudden" about sudden illumination. The trope of the unflappable Zen master and the earnest monk repeatedly missing the deep meaning of "the sound of one hand clapping" has, in its own way, become a part of the lore of Zen. Owing to the popular representations of the *kōan* and temple ordeals that have flowed from the works of Rinzai scholar D. T. Suzuki and his legion of Western followers, it may be that Rinzai is *the* Zen of the Western imagination, but the Sōtō school, founded by Dōgen, has been significantly larger than the Rinzai sect for most of its history.

Dōgen, like Eisai, entered the religious life as a child in Japan and later went to study Zen in China. His Chinese master, Rujing, a man of great piety and heroic asceticism, made a profound impression on Dōgen and inspired him to follow the Caodong path. After receiving the seal of transmission from Rujing, Dōgen returned to Japan and after a short time in residence at the Rinzai temple, Kenninji, established his own Sōtō community, Annyoin, near Kyoto. Dōgen, a more prolific scholar than Eisai, began writing the series of philosophical essays and practical instructions that would come to form the Zen classic *Shōbōgenzō,* the *Treasury of the True Dharma Eye.* Dōgen's body of work affirmed that the very practice of *zazen* was tantamount to achieving enlightenment. In other words, for Dōgen, Zen was not a matter of sitting or solving *kōan* for the sake of gaining awakening as a prize at the end. Rather, Zen *was* the practice of sitting, specifically sitting in the *shikantaza* position (the traditional lotus position), and the practice itself was the only prize one needed.

Zen temples continued to increase in number and size throughout the Kamakura period, receiving an influx of new blood in the middle of the thirteenth century as Chinese monks fled the Song empire during the Mongol wars. As the Five Mountain system ensured the continuing support of the *bakufu* and regularized the practices of the sect, Zen monks began to make the same kind of impact on Japanese cultural life that Chan literati had made on the cultural life of the Song. In the next chapter, we will look at the maturation of Zen aesthetics during the Muromachi period (1333–1573), a time in which warrior and Zen culture reached a peak of excellence.

6

Muromachi: The Apex of
Zen Warrior Culture

Daisetsu Teitaro (D. T.) Suzuki wrote, "In those days we can say that the Japanese genius went either to priesthood or to soldiery."[1] The days to which Suzuki was referring were the days of Japan's Muromachi period (1333–1573), when the Ashikaga, a family of priests and soldiers, ruled Japan during the highest flowering of Zen culture. As we saw in chapter 5, the convergence of Zen and the warrior ethos of the Kamakura regime at the turn of the thirteenth century heralded, after the end of the Heian period, a new period of vigor, self-discipline, and resolute action. By 1333, when the Ashikaga took control of the country after a brief political upheaval, Zen culture and the warrior aristocracy had both matured to the point that their seasoned confluence would produce a rich, multifaceted culture whose effects still resonate in the imaginations of people around the world.

The Muromachi period produced the first widespread articulations of what has come to be known as *bushidō,* the "way of the warrior," deriving from local samurai "house codes" and reinforced by layers of custom and legality that spelled out the sacred duties of warriors to their lords and the obligations of lords to their subjects. This period also saw the emergence of Noh theater, ink painting, calligraphy, and haiku and the maturation of the aesthetic ideals of *wabi* (the beauty of "fadedness") and *sabi* (the beauty of loneliness). All of these phenomena drew direct inspiration from Zen spirituality, and they are considered by many art historians to be the purest expressions of Japanese aesthetics. Zen reached its premodern apex hand in hand with warrior culture and fell from cultural dominance only when the *bakufu* itself fell into ruin during the prolonged period of civil war known as *sengoku.* By the time the "period of warring states" was over, the Ashikaga shogunate was all but irrelevant, and Zen's place of privilege in the minds of ruling elites had been usurped by another Chinese import, neo-Confucianism.

In determining which came first, samurai or Zen culture, we have to acknowledge that they clearly shaped each other, but since we see no similar relationship between the warrior class and Chan culture in China, it seems safe to say that it was the political clout of the warrior dynasties, emerging in the unique conditions of post-Heian Japan, both in Kamakura and Muromachi, that elevated Zen to the place of prominence that allowed it to exercise so much influence over Japanese high culture. The affection of the elite warriors for Zen was not accidental. As was noted briefly in chapter 5, Zen's various qualities were uniquely appealing to the samurai class. As Suzuki observes, Zen is a form of religious expression that favors discipline, simplicity, clarity, and directness, attributes also possessed by good warriors. Moreover, since life and death were of equal value to the Zen Buddhist, the warrior could gain from Zen a sense of serene confidence under the most dangerous of circumstances without becoming paralyzed by doubt or second-guessing. The Hōjō and Ashikaga clans did not merely permit the practice of Zen in Japan—they sometimes practiced it themselves.

The Hōjō ruled Japan for over a century, delegating a high degree of autonomy to their junior vassals and creating one of the most workable law codes in history (the Jōei Code of 1232). The Hōjō shoguns also effectively thwarted two Mongol invasions, which occurred, respectively, in 1274 and 1281. A ferocious typhoon stopped the Mongols in their second attempt to conquer Japan, and this great stroke of luck spared the inhabitants of the archipelago from a fate that few peoples, from Baghdad to Nanjing, were able to avoid. Fearing additional invasion attempts, the Kamakura government committed significant resources in treasure and manpower to keeping the southwest coast defended against an attack that never came. These defenses taxed the regime economically and politically, as numerous vassals became disgruntled over having to defend Japan's "national" borders when their chief concerns were with their own domains. In an atmosphere of weakening legitimacy, the Hōjō faced a revolt in the form of an ambitious emperor, Go-Daigo, who launched a short-lived but successful attempt to topple the *bakufu* and restore imperial power. In the Kenmu Restoration of 1333, the emperor exploited the various strains of dissatisfaction with the Hōjō, in particular the animosity of the Ashikaga family, whose chief, Takauji served as Go-Daigo's commanding general in the coup. After failing to reward Takauji with the office of shogun, and underestimating the power of the samurai families, Go-Daigo soon found himself opposed by Takauji, who ultimately forced the emperor's abdication and exile after only three years. Takauji then established his own capital in Kyoto and assumed control of the country, giving Japan an almost uninterrupted period of warrior government between 1185 and 1867.

The growth of the Zen sect, even during Go-Daigo's restoration, continued unabated. The emperor himself was a student of Zen and sponsored the construction of Daitokuji in 1324, which became one of Japan's most illustrious Zen temples. The Ashikaga were also committed patrons of Zen monasticism and used the nation's temples as command and control networks during their consolidation of the realm after deposing Go-Daigo. Tenryūji built in 1339, was intended by Takauji to serve as a memorial to the exiled emperor—a symbol of atonement, perhaps, for betraying his onetime imperial lord. Tenryūji would be included, along with several other new temples, in an expanded register of *gozan*, or "Five Mountain" temples. As noted in chapter 5, the Five Mountain system in the Kamakura period consisted of five original Rinzai temples in Kamakura: Kenchōji, Jōchiji, Engakuji, Jomyoji, and Jufukuji. Go-Daigo, in a move aimed at placing Kamakura's Zen establishment below Kyoto's, added Daitokuji and Nanzenji. Daitokuji was later removed from the final list, which was only consolidated in 1386 after the dedication of the Shōkokuji temple. Under the new list, authorized by the shogun Yoshimitsu (1367–95), Kyoto and Kamakura each had five ranked temples of "mountain" status, with an eleventh, Nanzenji, designated as the "first" temple of the realm, a kind of flagship temple for the entire system:

	Kyoto	Kamakura
First rank	Tenryūji	Kenchōji
Second rank	Shōkokuji	Engakuji
Third rank	Kenninji	Jufukuji
Fourth rank	Tōfukuji	Jōchiji
Fifth rank	Manjuji	Jomyoji

Beneath the *gozan* temples were over sixty regional temples, called *jissatsu*, and below these were hundreds of smaller provincial temples, all of which served in various religious, cultural, and administrative capacities for the shogunate. In addition to occasionally helping the Ashikaga communicate policy to the far-flung provinces, these temples also served an external diplomatic function as communication and exchanges with the Chinese Chan communities continued throughout the Mongol occupation in China. When the Ming overthrew the Mongols in 1368, Yoshimitsu wasted no time declaring his fealty to the new Chinese dynasty, and he used the good offices of the Zen temples to make the necessary contacts.

The *gozan* system owed much of its administrative effectiveness to Musō Kokushi (1275–1351), the remarkable abbot of Tenryūji and one of the most energetic and learned priests of the era. As head of the chief Kyoto temple, he spearheaded the building of numerous local temples throughout Japan. These temples, established for the "pacification of the nation," not only projected *bakufu* power into the hinterlands, but they also helped popularize the Zen sect among rural commoners. While Zen would never approach the popularity of such sects as the Pure Land, it did gain adherents across class lines and outside the urban centers of power. The popularization of Zen fortunately did not promote the widespread laxity that had afflicted such schools as the Tendai during the Heian period. Musō's "admonition" to the monasteries is evidence of the abbot's desire to keep monastic discipline tight and religious fervor strong when broad expansion and rapid secularization might have threatened the integrity of the religious life. He wrote, "[T]hose minds that are intoxicated by secular literature and engaged in establishing themselves as men of letters and are simply laymen with shaven heads . . . do not even belong to the lowest [grade of disciples]."[2]

During this expansive period, the Zen monasteries became hubs of creative activity, visited by retreating court nobles and retired warrior aristocrats who helped turn the temples from meditation halls into great centers of learning and cultural production. The temples cultivated a wide range of martial and fine arts, including many of the artistic forms that have come down to us through the centuries as quintessential modes of Japanese culture, among them Zen gardening, ink painting, and the tea ceremony.

Looking at these phenomena, literally from the ground up, Musō himself may be ranked among the first master gardeners of the Zen landscaping tradition. His gardens clearly depict the fusion of accepting the "suchness" of reality with pushing beyond the limits of reality that has always defined the complex Zen attitude toward nature. His garden at Tenryūji, for example, which is dominated by the natural beauty of a large woodland pond, also features a carefully constructed arrangement of rocks that symbolizes the wild beauty of the Chinese mountains where Zen was born. Musō's garden, Saihōji, shows even more clearly the degree to which nature can be shaped into the form of a truly unearthly ideal. Walking over a lush green carpet of cultivated moss to a man-made pond fashioned in the shape of the Japanese character *shin* (meaning "mind" or "heart"), a disciple finds the image of peace and mindfulness literally inscribed on the natural environment. The clear message of these gardens is that the beauty of nature is only enhanced by the intentionality of the gardener, which is ideally reproduced in the contemplative intentionality of each person who meditates there.

Many Zen gardeners replaced the ponds with water-free representations of ponds, rivers, waterfalls, and even oceans. The *kare-sansui*, or "dry landscape," which uses pebbles and sand in place of water, has become, perhaps, the signature feature of the Zen garden. Kogaku Soko's Daisenin garden at Daitokuji temple includes a stone river, raked into ripples that vividly suggest the fluid movement of a river coursing toward the sea. The most celebrated dry landscape is the rock garden at Ryōanji temple in Kyoto. This seemingly random arrangement of fifteen rock "islands" in an ocean of sand has become an emblem not only of Zen aesthetics but, in the minds of some modern art historians, the very essence of Japan itself. The contemplative function of these gardens, we could say, is to use less to suggest more, a gesture that serves meditation by taking the disciple beyond reliance on substance and toward surrender to the mystery of the formless.

Figure 6.1. The Zen garden at Ryōanji Temple, Kyoto, Japan.

The highly constructed beauty of these gardens may inspire the curious student to ask why nature, if it is regarded so highly by the Zen monk, has to be so strictly controlled and constructed. Would it not be more "Zen" to leave nature alone? Suzuki, in *Zen and Japanese Culture,* alludes to this problem, concluding:

Beauty is felt when there is freedom of motion and freedom of expression. Beauty is not in form but in the meaning it expresses, and this meaning is felt when the observing subject throws his whole being into the bearer of the meaning and moves along with it. This is possible only when he lives in a "superworld" where no mutually excluding oppositions take place, or rather when the mutually excluding oppositions of which we are always too conscious in this world of multiplicities are taken up even as they are into something of a higher order than they. Aestheticism now merges into religion.[3]

We might conclude, then, that the construction of the garden is in the purest sense a religious experience and that the transformation of the landscape through meditative gardening is in some real way analogous to the transformation of the self through *zazen.* A Zen monk would be no more satisfied with an uncultivated garden than with an unenlightened mind.

Some historians see the Zen garden as a three-dimensional replica of the kind of religious "superworlds" depicted in the landscapes of the Zen *sumi-e* (ink painters). The tradition of monochrome painting can be traced to such Song dynasty Chan artists as Muqi and Mayuan, who first mastered the minimalist but spiritually evocative technique of ink and wash on paper. The aesthetic aim of Zen painting is to suggest, with the merest brush stroke, as much as possible of the underlying mystery of nature or the hidden depths of character in human—or even animal—subjects. Among the exemplary works of this genre are *Winter Landscape* by Sesshū Toyo (1420–1506) and *Reading in the Bamboo Study* by Tenshō Shūbun (d. ca. 1450), both of Shōkokuji temple in Kyoto. The most interesting feature of all of these pieces, at least from the standpoint of Zen, is not the degree to which they stand as works of art but more the degree to which they serve as aids to meditation. One can sit before a Sesshū painting, in the same way one recites a sutra or contemplates a *kōan*, using it to move beyond the self into the void of *prajñāpāramitā*—adding a dimension of richness and aesthetic satisfaction to the contemplative experience.

This property is even more impressive in the case of objects that are produced for practical use, in particular, tea ceramics, which are meant not only for the functional purpose of serving tea but also for helping the participant use the tea ceremony, or *cha no yū*, as a means of leaving the mundane world behind. The great tea master Sen no Rikyū established the standards of the Muromachi tea ceremony, both ritually and aesthetically. According to Rikyū, tea bowls should be prized not for their perfection of shape or homogeneity of color but for their imperfections. The most beautiful bowl was one that exhibited an odd shape or irregular color. As participants went through the careful rituals of tea preparation, service, and drinking, they entered into a relationship with the bitter tea, and the utensils as well, entering a zone that for many devotees was a threshold between earth and the Buddha fields. The quirkiness and rustic plainness of the bowls helped this journey by making palpably real two critical ideals of Zen art, *wabi*, and *sabi*, aesthetic values that point to the quiet mind because they tend to arrest the mind from its occupation with control, organization, and the human desire to keep death and sorrow at bay. *Wabi* refers to the beauty of fadedness, even shabbiness, and calls forth the delight that one can take in something that has aged with grace and elegance. *Sabi*, on the other hand, is the beauty possessed by something sad, lonely, or forlorn—a tree that has lost its leaves in winter or a building that bears the marks of neglect; these are things that evoke a certain pathos indicative of life's ultimate ephemeral nature.

The properties of *wabi* and *sabi*, are clear in the architecture of the spare and rustic tearoom itself. In a real way, the consecrated space of the tearoom enjoys a kinship with meditative sanctuaries of all kinds; it is the descendant of Bodhidharma's cave, the huts of Tang dynasty mendicants, and the mountain sanctuaries of Daoist recluses. In medieval Japan, the hut has its own history as a locus of political dissent. Kamo no Chōmei's *Ten Square Foot Hut* is, in part, an early anthem of resistance to the Heian court as corruption and instability began to shake its ancient foundations. Yoshida Kenkō, another author who adopts the trope of the recluse, but in good Muromachi Zen fashion, embraces the instability and uncertainty of life as a positive value. This passage from Yoshida's *Essays in Idleness* is as clear an homage to *wabi* and *sabi* as one can find in the literature of the period.

> Somebody once remarked that thin silk was not satisfactory as a scroll wrapping because it was so easily torn. Ton'a replied, "It is only after the silk wrapper has frayed at top and bottom, and the mother-of-pearl has fallen from the roller that a scroll looks beautiful." This opinion demonstrated the excellent taste of the man. People often say that a set of books looks ugly if all of the volumes are not in the same format, but I was impressed to hear the Abbot Kōyū say, "It is typical of the unintelligent man to insist on assembling complete sets of everything. Incomplete sets are better.[4]

On the topic of irregular sets, no discussion of Muromachi Zen aesthetics would be adequate without some mention of the two most celebrated works of Ashikaga architecture, namely, Kinkakuji, the Golden Pavilion built by the shogun Yoshimitsu in 1397, and the Silver Pavilion, Ginkakuji, built by his grandson Yoshimasa in 1482. These were intended as sanctuaries for their respective patrons, but Kinkakuji, a stunning palace resplendent with gold leaf, reflects the personality of a ruler at the height of power. Ginkakuji, a rustic estate complete with a tearoom that fairly drips with the spirit of *wabi*, seems more the creation of a shogun in retreat from strife, having lost control of a troubled realm, and whose glory days were receding into the past.

Yoshimasa, more an aesthete than a warrior, cared little for military matters or managing the state. It was he who precipitated the Ōnin War by changing his designated heir, touching off a bitter war of succession. Ten years after the war's outbreak in 1467, the capital was left in ruins, and the urban violence was exported to the countryside as clan chiefs repaired to their respective domains to carve out spheres of influence in a long period of warfare and treachery that would last over a century. While the Ashikaga continued to "reign" in Kyoto, neither they nor any other of the 250 or so feudal domain chiefs, or daimyo, were able to exert any real political control over the fragmented Japanese archipelago. The central influence of the shogunate and

Figure 6.2. Shogun Ashikaga Yoshimitsu (1358–1408).

the religious influence of the Five Mountain system would both be eclipsed as power shifted to the rural periphery. In chapter 7, we will see that the decline of the *bakufu* would be something analogous to the decline of the Middle Ages in Europe, when religious dominance gave ground to new definitions of the state and society, reinforced by new state-centered political philosophies. While Zen culture would continue to thrive among the warrior elites, it would never again enjoy the influence it commanded when it was—at least in some sense—the "official" religion of the Ashikaga *bakufu*.

7

ZEN'S CHALLENGE TO THE
MODERN WORLD

The unification of Japan under Tokugawa Ieyasu brought an end to the medieval synthesis of Zen and warrior culture. The Tokugawa *bakufu* was itself a warrior government, but the defining feature of this *bakufu* was its success in eradicating warfare and creating the conditions that would allow Japan to enjoy over two centuries of general peace. Ironically, a warrior government reigned while warfare was, for all intents and purposes, abolished. As for Zen, the monastic communities survived, and maintained ties to the government, but the relationship increasingly became one of state control rather than state patronage.

Many historians refer to the Tokugawa, or Edo, period (1603–1867) as Japan's "early modern" age, suggesting that it is a precursor of the Meiji era's (1867–1912) political centralization, capitalism, and social reorganization rather than merely a continuation of Muromachi feudalism. Whether this interpretation is correct or not has been an ongoing debate among Japanese historians. Nevertheless, when Japan was confronted in the nineteenth century with a choice to modernize or face possible colonial subjugation, it managed to adopt, adapt, and reinvent the external forms of Western civilization with astonishing speed, and in less than fifty years moved to the front rank of modern world powers. Zen played an important role in Japan's modernization, emerging from a long period of comparative stagnation in the Edo period to serve as a vital cultural force in the more cosmopolitan Meiji era. What follows is a brief account of Zen's development in both the Tokugawa and Meiji eras and how it influenced Japan's redefinition of itself as a "modern" society.

The central concern of the early Tokugawa shogunate was to preserve peace after over a century of civil war. The *bakufu* implemented authoritarian policies designed to regulate the identity, social mobility, economic production, and even day-to-day activities of Japan's various classes. To establish for itself the legitimacy needed for this radical overhaul of society, the shogunate appropriated the neo-Confucianism of Zhuxi (1130–1200), a Song dynasty scholar whose political philosophy redefined the relationship between state and society throughout the East Asian region for several centuries. Adapting Zhuxi's political and social theories to their particular circumstances, Tokugawa court scholars promoted the idea of a social order based on a sacred hierarchy leading directly from heaven all the way down to the lowest commoner. The key element of this structure was the shogun, who ruled over the earthly order and mediated its fragile negotiation with the divine realm. In order to keep the cosmos in harmony, it was essential that all members of society fulfill their roles and carry out their appointed duties. We can see then that the Tokugawa regime did not think of religion in the same way that the Ashikaga did, as a cultural branch of the realm that assisted in implementing policy. Under the Tokugawa, religion was considered an ideological foundation for the reinforcement of state power.

Accordingly, any locus of power or legitimacy outside the state was seen as a threat to good order and was ruthlessly eliminated. Christianity, which made its appearance in 1549, was brutally suppressed, as were many of the Buddhist communities during the unification. As was the case in Tang China, Zen managed to survive the worst of the persecutions, although its prestige and cultural influence were both much reduced.

During the latter part of the Warring States period, Zen experienced a general decline that mirrored the political fortunes of the Ashikaga shogunate. The most celebrated Zen master of the late Muromachi period, Ikkyū, did not achieve fame for his piety or holy profundity but rather for his worldly irreverence. This brazen poet-monk was notorious for breaking monastic rules and scandalizing his superiors with scathing criticism of their hypocrisies, to say nothing of openly indulging his appetite for sake and prostitutes. After a falling-out with a fellow monk, he left his monastery and became an itinerant priest, living for a time with a minstrel woman named Mori. Among his best-known "religious" poems are songs of praise for male and female sexual organs! For all his eccentricities, he was revered as a true holy man whose carefree lifestyle revealed evidence of a genuine, if not exactly pristine, awakening.

Throughout the seventeenth century, Zen continued to descend from its former heights of cultural glory. Aside from the introduction of the Ōbaku sect from China in 1661, there were few new movements in Zen monastic life or innovations in doctrinal interpretation. The spirit of the age lay not in the Zen ethos of the warrior elites but rather in the urban entertainments of the merchant classes. In contrast to the refined Ashikaga arts of ink painting and the tea ceremony, the Tokugawa period saw the popularization of sumo wrestling, Kabuki theater, and licensed brothels. Even the *Hagakure*, an early-eighteenth-century classic on *bushidō*—the so-called way of the samurai—by Yamamoto Tsunetomo, seems to be more of a nostalgic fabrication of a warrior code that never existed than an embodiment of a living samurai culture.

In the eighteenth century, an incipient form of Japanese national identity emerged as new discourses of nativism increased awareness of Japan's indigenous religious traditions. The Kokugaku, or "National Learning," movement was initiated by scholars such as Motoori Norinaga, who studied Japan's mythical past and found evidence of an essential Japaneseness in the tales and religious customs of antiquity. Norinaga's central aesthetic ideal, *mono no aware* (the pathos of things) celebrated the poignant beauty of transient phenomena and identified sensitivity to ephemeral beauty as a defining Japanese trait. By the nineteenth century, the National Learning movement would contribute to a reconceptualization of Shintō, Japan's ancient "way of the gods," as the core of a spiritual ideology that best expressed the cultural values of the Japanese people. Yet because the idea of *mono no aware* exhibits such a clear resonance with the aesthetic ideals of Zen Buddhism, the cultural nationalists of Japan's modern period had little difficulty drawing Zen, despite its "foreign" roots, into the construction of a protomodern national consciousness.

Japan's early modern nationalism was somewhat different from its counterparts in Europe in that it tended to connect religious identity to national identity rather than reducing it to a second-tier status below political subjecthood. This made the rise of early modern nationalism in Japan as much a religious renewal as a political innovation, and all of Japan's religious traditions, native or "foreign," would play a role in the shaping of national identity. Zen's most significant contribution to intellectual renewal in the Tokugawa era was the work of Hakuin, the greatest master of the period. A brilliant, multitalented, and devout mystic, Hakuin reinvigorated the practice of *kōan* meditation and urged his disciples to commit themselves fully to *zazen*, as he himself did, often going days without sleep. His "Song of Meditation" is still revered as one of the greatest scriptures of the Zen tradition.

> The Zen meditation of the Mahayana is beyond all praise.
> Giving and morality and the other perfections,
> Taking of the Name, repentance and discipline
> And the many other right actions
> All come back to the practice of meditation
> By the merit of a single sitting
> He destroys innumerable accumulated sins.[1]

The National Learning movement, because of its valorization of ancient traditions, ultimately served as a destabilizing force during the Tokugawa regime. By the mid–nineteenth century, the *bakufu* was contending with economic crisis, social unrest, and brewing political rebellion, as an increasing number of samurai began to argue that Japan's emperor, who had long played only a marginal role in political life but was acknowledged as both a high priest and deity in the Shinto tradition, should be restored to his ancient role as Japan's sovereign king. General dissatisfaction with the *bakufu* hardened into specific anger when foreign powers began to defy a long-standing isolation policy and sent merchant ships in to penetrate Japan's quarantined coastline. The American commodore Matthew Perry delivered an 1853 ultimatum that forced Japan to open its borders to Western trade and diplomacy. The 1854 Treaty of Kanagawa, granting the United States access to the ports of Hakodate and Shimoda, triggered an alarmed nativist reaction under the banner of *sonnō joi* (revere the emperor, expel the barbarian), which led in turn to the toppling of the Tokugawa shogunate by a group of rebellious samurai in 1868.

The revolutionaries who brought down the *bakufu* quickly shifted to a pro-Western stance, believing that cooperation with the West, and the modernization of Japan's economy and military forces, would buy them enough time to strengthen their position and ensure their country's independence. Under the ostensible rule of the young Meiji emperor, the new government enacted a sweeping range of reforms and sent officials abroad to learn modern technologies in the hopes that Japan could "catch up" to the West and deal with America and Europe on equal terms. It was, ironically, in this determined rush to modernize that the ancient way of Zen acquired new importance in Japanese culture.

In the first few years of the Meiji era, Buddhism suffered persecution as the ruling clique tried to establish neo-Shinto emperor veneration as a state ideology. What became clear to many of the officials who had gone abroad, though, was that *proper* modern states practiced freedom of religion. In the mid-1870s, the Japanese government relaxed its anti-Buddhist stance, although it continued to stress the duties of all Japanese to venerate the emperor. Meiji Japan thus gave birth to an odd system of religious toleration in which people were free to practice any religion they chose, as long as it was understood that they were also inherently Shinto by virtue of their nationality. "State Shinto," a quasi-state religion, remained the real orthodoxy of Japan until the end of World War II.

The Zen monasteries were careful to stay on the good side of the state as they took advantage of unprecedented religious freedom. Monks traveled abroad and entered into religious dialogues with colleagues overseas. Shaku Sōen, the abbot of Engakuji temple in Kamakura, was perhaps the most adventurous Zen monk of the period. In 1893, he accepted an invitation to attend the World Parliament of Religions in Chicago, marking the debut of Zen in the United States. Unlike his spiritual predecessor Bodhidharma, Sōen did not try to befuddle anybody with cryptic answers to simple questions, and he did not serve up enigmatic *kōan*, violent "*katsu*" strikes, or paradoxical silences to the delegates at the parliament. His paper, "The Law of Cause and Effect as Taught by the Buddha," was a "matter-of-fact and down-to-earth" speech that made references to modern science and appealed to the practical

Figure 7.1. The Zen monk, Shaku Sōen.

logic of the Western mind.[2] Sōen was trying *not* to appear as an Eastern mystic but rather as someone who understood the modern world and wanted to show that Zen was fully compatible with it. Because Sōen spoke no English, his paper was read by an interpreter using a text that D. T. Suzuki, at the time a young lay monk at Engakuji, had translated.

Among the attendees at the parliament was Dr. Paul Carus, an oriental scholar who was impressed by Sōen and asked him to stay in Illinois to help him translate a collection of Buddhist texts. Unfortunately for Carus, the abbot had to return to Engakuji, but instead he sent Suzuki, who would spend the following nine years in America. Working as Carus's houseboy by day and translating Buddhist texts by night, Suzuki produced an impressive number of translations, which brought the teachings of Mahāyāna and Zen to the attention of American readers. Unknown to Suzuki, as he toiled away in Illinois producing the first English Buddhist canon, back in Japan, Zen was being transformed into a modern national religion. The Parliament of World Religions had placed Japanese culture on the map, right at the time when Japanese military forces were also gaining the respect of the world. With stunning victories over China in 1895 and Russia in 1905, Japan demonstrated its preeminence among nations in Asia. The heady experience of being the first—and at that point only—modern state in Asia convinced Japanese cultural elites that there was something unique about their nation's historical development. As proud Japanese scholars scoured history for evidence of their nation's special qualities, they determined that Zen was among the essential ingredients of authentic Japanese culture. Thus, Zen became not only a part of Japan's claim to universal legitimacy as a great modern state but also a rationale for a new burst of nativist pride.

In the early twentieth century, a new generation of Japanese thinkers grappled with the meaning of Japan's historical destiny. Among the more provocative interpreters of Japan's complex relationship between the "world-universal" and the "cultural-particular" was Nishida Kitarō, Japan's first great philosopher of the modern age. Nishida became a Zen Buddhist in 1896, having been introduced to *zazen* by his friend D. T. Suzuki while they were both students at Tokyo University. After his awakening in 1903, Nishida worked systematically to integrate the "irrational" features of Zen dialectics—being and nonbeing, substance and nothingness, and so on—into a modern rational philosophy of metaphysics, epistemology, and history. One of Nishida's innovations was to reinterpret the history of the world as a dialectical process in which individual nations interacted with the larger world in a series of mutual "self-negations," meaning that nations and the world were constantly "emptying" themselves for each other as history unfolded. At the end of the

56

historical process lay what Nishida called "absolute nothingness," a kind of world-level Zen awakening at the end of history. Nishida was not the first philosopher to suggest that the world was moving toward some kind of historical fulfillment, but his description of this fulfillment in metaphysical Zen terms brought Zen a new intellectual respectability as the underlying logic of a fully articulated historical philosophy.

After 1931, the year in which Japan conquered Manchuria and opened a fifteen-year war of aggression in China, an increasing number of Japanese became concerned with the problem of history and the question of their nation's role in the world. Throughout the 1930s, Japanese universities and newspapers fell largely in line with the government's militaristic goals, serving in some cases as organs of propaganda for the "Imperial Way." The army, which had bristled under Japan's inferior status throughout the Meiji era, welcomed its new place in the world with satisfaction. Emphasizing the centrality of emperor worship to the Japanese "national essence," state and military authorities created a new orthodoxy that exalted the throne and justified Japan's invasions as the appropriate acts of a sacred land in the pacification of lawless states. The Zen monasteries were openly supportive of expansion in China and helped foster a contrived revival of *bushido* in the modern-day imperial army. The emergence of what was called "Imperial Way Zen" shows the degree to which Zen can be, and has been, appropriated for any number of dubious modern uses. When we consider the ease with which the Japanese government "drafted" Zen for the sake of promulgating nationalism in the 1930s, it may strike us as odd, if not ominous, that at the same time a growing number of westerners were also turning to Zen out of a sense of disillusionment with their own culture.

World War I was a true turning point in the history of modern consciousness. Despite celebrating rationalism, equality, and freedom as universal values, the modern Enlightenment civilization of Europe had actually substantially contributed to world economic misery, social injustice, racial inequality, and imperialism, all of which were causes of the carnage of the "Great War." The colonized masses of Asia and Africa already felt that Western modernity provided satisfaction only to a select few—but when westerners also began to question the assumptions of their own civilization, it seemed that a moment of crisis had been reached. Many Europeans and Americans turned to Asian philosophy and religion as a means of finding some way out of the catastrophe that modern material progress seemed to have visited on the world. Such books as *Essays in Zen Buddhism* (1927), *An Introduction to Zen Buddhism* (1934), *A Manual of Zen Buddhism* (1934), and *The Training of the Zen Buddhist Monk* (1934), all authored by D. T. Suzuki, gave

Figure 7.2. Alan Watts, D.T. Suzuki, and Christmas Humphreys, 1958.
Photo by Lawrence Watts.

many in the West their first taste of an alternative spirituality. Suzuki rapidly became known as Zen's foremost apostle to Europe and North America.

Suzuki had returned to Japan in 1909, and he spent several decades thereafter teaching, writing, and publishing an international journal called the *Eastern Buddhist*. In response to an invitation from the organizers of the World Congress of Faiths, Suzuki traveled to London in 1936 and saw the abundant fruits that his scholarship had yielded in the mission fields of the West. Congress organizers included Christmas Humphreys, an attorney from the London Buddhist Lodge, and a prodigy named Alan Watts, who at the age of twenty had already made enough of a mark on the English Buddhist community to be selected as the discussant for Suzuki's paper. Humphreys and Watts would make leading contributions to the field of western Zen studies well into the post–World War II era and never lost their conviction that Zen had something to offer Western civilization that its overemphasis on materialism had placed out of reach. As Humphreys wrote in 1949:

> Few doubt today that the west has need of a new enlightenment, which means that the old light, for the Light is one, is in need of a new expression. Our vaunted science changes its mind repeatedly, exchanging last month's final conclusions for those of the last; and its discoveries are handed over, with the gesture of washing the hands of all responsibility, to those whose ambition and livelihood it is to kill their fellow men. Religion too, has

failed in the hour of adversity. Two world wars have struck such a blow at Christianity as may prove mortal; truth may be deathless but its forms must die. It is just because Zen has no form which it is not willing on the least occasion to discard that it is immortal, for it is a wine that will use any bottle that comes in handy, or will make new bottles of its own. With the failure of Christianity, enquiring minds have sought new outlets for the religious sentiments of the mind.[3]

When we consider this statement in light of the deep antagonism felt by westerners toward Japan during World War II, it only shows the degree to which Western religion had been discredited in the minds of at least some materialists and nonmaterialists alike. Humphreys's characterization of Zen as an exclusively peaceful religion seems indicative of a sincere love of Zen but inaccurate understanding of its historical affinity with the Japanese military. His claim that "there has never been a 'Buddhist,' still less to use that blasphemous phrase, a 'holy' Buddhist, war," seems a bit naive when we look more closely at the activities and declarations of prominent Zen Buddhists during the prosecution of Japan's war in China.[4]

Many Western Zen devotees had little idea, until fairly recently, of the degree to which Zen was involved in Japanese militarism and the army establishment. *Zen at War,* by Brian Victoria, revealed some of the unpleasant truths about the latter-day Zen "samurai." Victoria's study shows the deep institutional connections between the Zen establishment and the modern Japanese army that reinforced Japanese imperialism throughout the war. Not only did many Buddhist generals of the imperial army consider it appropriate for the Zen temples to support the pacification of "barbarian" nations (such as China!), but they argued that the execution of military duties in service of the state was equivalent to a religious act. Suzuki himself, who lived in Japan and published throughout the war, was an outspoken nationalist, although he quickly atoned at the end of the war.

During the Occupation of Japan, Suzuki was sought out at his home by several American servicemen who had read his works during their training as military interpreters. They encouraged him to come out of retirement, and soon afterward he accepted invitations to speak in Hawaii, California, and New York. He eventually took up a visiting faculty position at Columbia University, where he began what was arguably the most fruitful phase of his long career. Playing the role of Zen sage, complete with kimono and sandals, Suzuki held forth on the dharma in college lectures, church sermons, magazine interviews, and television talk shows. He quickly found himself the toast of New York's cultural establishment and could list as his friends such luminaries as Carl Jung, W. T. de Bary, Thomas Merton, John Cage, and

Huston Smith. His books were reprinted in paperback and became so well known among the American literati that Zen became one of the bywords of progressive urban culture. Ruth Fuller Sasaki, an ordained monk who is often considered the "matron" of American Zen, made the following observation in 1959:

> Zen has always been credited with influencing Far Eastern Art, but now the discovery has been made that it was existing all along in English literature. Ultramodern painting, music, dance, and poetry are acclaimed as expressions of Zen. Zen is invoked to substantiate the latest theories in psychology, psychotherapy, philosophy, semantics, mysticism, free thinking, and what-have-you. It is the magic word at smart cocktail parties and bohemian get-togethers alike.[5]

The Western Zen boom that began in the 1950s brought great satisfaction to Suzuki, as it seemed to redeem Japanese culture from damages sustained during World War II. It also offered the promise that an ancient Asian religious tradition could make real contributions to a modern historical consciousness that had been weakened by the tragic events of the first half of the twentieth century. In the concluding chapter of this story, we will examine how Zen fared in the latter half of the twentieth century and raise a question or two about its prospects for the future.

8

From Dharma Bums
to Punk Zen

Daisetsu Teitaro (D. T.) Suzuki's pilgrimage to New York marked the beginning of a multifaceted relationship between Zen and postwar American culture, several aspects of which we will explore in this chapter. Before we begin, though, we should pause for a moment and consider the odd reality that only ten years after World War II—a conflict in which Japan and America fought to the finish over radically divergent views about state, society, and culture—a conservative Japanese scholar should become the spiritual mentor of some of the most liberal intellectuals in America. We should remember, too, that Zen, which served in the Meiji era as one of Japan's claims to modern legitimacy, was used during the war as an ideological weapon to "overcome" the modern world. Zen's divided identity would continue throughout the postwar era; not only would Zen become the focus of spiritual aspiration for successive generations of middle-class wisdom seekers, but it would also inform a wide range of "postmodern" cultural and academic movements. That Zen should be used as both an argument *for* and an argument *against* the validity of modern historical consciousness is perhaps consistent with its essentially paradoxical nature, but it has thrown contemporary understandings of Zen, as was noted in Chapter 1, into some confusion. It may be that the great historical paradox is not Zen but modernity itself!

In July 1942, a group of Japanese intellectuals was invited by the Kyoto Literary Society to take part in its "Symposium on Overcoming Modernity." The purpose of this conference was to articulate ways in which the Pacific War might enable Japan to transcend modern Western civilization. The attendees wanted to open a kind of intellectual front in Japan's "holy war" against British, American, and Dutch imperialism.[1] Among the participants were several of Nishida Kitarō's disciples, scholars who were steeped in his Zen-based worldview of "absolute nothingness" and shared his view that Japanese culture, in fulfilling its particular destiny, would help bring about the transformation of the historical world. One of these disciples was Nishitani Keiji, a Zen scholar whose paper argued that the crisis in world history could be attributed to the combined effects of the Renaissance and Reformation, which drove a wedge between the spiritual and material understandings of reality in the Western mind.

According to Nishitani, the separation between spirit and nature, God and humanity, and so on, had led to the triumph of science in the modern world and reduced the religious life to merely a cultural by-product. It was bad enough that modern secularism had divided the consciousness of Western Europe, but as European civilization came to dominate the entire world through imperialism, even East Asia suffered under the spirit-deadening effects of modern consciousness. The way for Japan to overcome modernity, said Nishitani, was to revitalize its religious life and redefine the meaning of the individual from the "standpoint of subjective nothingness."[2] Nishitani believed that when the West was defeated (which in July 1942 still seemed possible) Japan, the purest example of a Zen nation, would lead the world into a new religious age.

As we know, Japan lost World War II, mostly as a result of the overwhelming technology and raw power of the modern West's industrial output, a power demonstrated most horrifyingly with the deployment of two atomic weapons. It would seem that any debate on "overcoming the modern" was decisively resolved in this gesture except, as was the case after World War I, many intellectuals and even some political elites came to harbor serious concerns about the costs involved in preserving the modern world order. If the carnage of World War I was evidence that modern civilization had run off the rails, what was there to say about the unleashing of the atomic age? Japan, occupied by American forces, had no contribution to make concerning the plans for postwar global society. Its ideology was banished, and many of its intellectuals were branded as war criminals.

Nishida, who had often been accused by Japan's military government before the war of holding recklessly liberal and pro-Western tendencies, was vilified during the Occupation as an ultra-right-wing nationalist, and Nishitani was forced to resign from his Kyoto University professorship. In such purges of the academic establishment, it was hoped that all traces of the Japanese military mind-set, including Imperial Way Zen, would be erased from the popular consciousness. That Suzuki, a close friend and ideological comrade of both Nishida and Nishitani, was rehabilitated as a wise and kindly "oriental" sage in postwar America is curious to say the least, but it reflects the spiritual uncertainty that affected many Americans in the postwar years. Seeking refuge in the apparent normalcy of middle-class life and material aspirations, the United States created a culture of mass-produced everydayness and consumerism while the national government stockpiled nuclear weapons against the threat of its new mortal enemy, the Soviet Union.

In the 1950s, as the United States assumed its role as the guardian of modern civilization, culture prophets of various stripes began to weigh in with their judgments that all was not well in the Western world. Psychoanalysts such as Carl Jung and Erich Fromm, Catholic priests such as Thomas Merton, artists such as John Cage and Ad Reinhardt, and literati such as Jack Kerouac and Allen Ginsberg all challenged in their work the philosophical assumptions of bourgeois culture, as well as the absolutism of its rational order. They also raised, in their various ways, serious questions about the ability of modern materialism to provide humanity with a satisfactory future. What these voices in the wilderness shared in common, besides their incipient "postmodernism," was an affinity for Zen Buddhism, acquired through the works of D. T. Suzuki, who frankly stated that the modern world was "groping in the dark."[3] Although none of these people was a practicing Buddhist, they all thought that Zen might be part of a cure for a kind of historical sickness, an antidote to the poison that was beginning to consume, in their opinions, the death-obsessed, materialist, and consumer-driven society of postwar America. Merton, a contemplative monk, represented this perspective quite clearly with the following assertion.

> The impact of Zen on the West, striking with its fullest force right after World War II, in the midst of the existentialist upheaval, at the beginning of the atomic and cybernetic age, with Western religion and philosophy in a state of crisis and with consciousness of man threatened by the deepest alienation, the work and personal influence of Dr. Suzuki proved to be both timely and fruitful: much more fruitful than we have perhaps begun to realize.[4]

The beatniks were probably the most influential of the modernity critics because their works made the greatest impression on the popular culture. Jack Kerouac's *On the Road* and Allen Ginsberg's *Howl* enjoyed enormous readerships and came to serve as literary anthems of a new generation skeptical of the promises of the Western bourgeois establishment and eager to break free of its confines.

Kerouac learned about Buddhism through a translation of Ashvaghosha's biography of the Buddha. When he discovered the second Noble Truth of desire as the cause of suffering, he took the wisdom of this message to heart and made it something of a centerpiece for his writing career. As he explained, in the aftermath of a failed love affair, he vowed to embrace the dharma and spend his earthly life as a Buddhist "mendicant thinker."[5] Whether his alcohol- and drug-fueled forays across America with driving buddy Neal Cassady count as holy pilgrimages is debatable, but he did succeed in introducing millions of Americans to the vocabulary of Mahāyāna Buddhism. On a superficial level, the "Zen" of Kerouac, a hard-drinking, fast-living dropout from society, can be compared to that of the Muromachi Zen master Ikkyū, another wild spirit who became an aesthetic model for many Zen bohemians. While Kerouac was never a seriously practicing Buddhist, his voluminous *Some of the Dharma*, a journal of prayers, notes, and meditations, shows an attempt to infuse a seemingly hedonistic lifestyle with spiritual value. The most popular account of his engagement with Zen can be found in the autobiographical novel *Dharma Bums*, which memorializes the meeting between Ray Smith (Kerouac) and "Zen lunatic" Japhy Ryder in San Francisco in 1955. This Beat classic offers perhaps the best insight into the way the self-styled secular monks of American letters tried to reinvent lay Buddhism and shows how "dharma bums" such as Japhy saw Zen as an integral part of a new social and spiritual vision of America—complete with poetry, ecology, and a return to nature by way of a peacefully apocalyptic "rucksack revolution."

Japhy, the fictional Gary Snyder, emerges in the novel as the epitome of the simple, studious, and cheerfully eccentric lay Zen monk, moving easily through any environment with only a backpack (containing a copy of Suzuki's essays, of course) and a few simple belongings. This is an accurate enough depiction of the young Snyder, who would mature into a legitimate Zen scholar, a distinguished academic, and a Pulitzer prize–winning poet. Like Kerouac and Ginsberg, Snyder also discovered Zen through the works of Suzuki, but unlike his Beat comrades, he went on to study Zen formally as a novice at the Shōkokuji temple in Kyoto. Although Kerouac is universally recognized as the icon of the Beat generation, Snyder can probably be credited with having done more to engineer the confluence of modern Zen with popular culture than any of the part-time Buddhists in the Beat movement. As the exemplary backpacking, haiku-composing, and Zen-meditating beatnik, Snyder became the living prototype of the earnest hippie seeker of the following decade.

The most controversial of Zen's various cultural entanglements was undoubtedly its dynamic but short-lived kinship with psychedelic drugs in the 1950s and early 1960s. In the mid-1950s, LSD was being used, legally, by a small group of intellectuals and artists, who marveled at its ability to shatter perceptions, destroy ego obsession, and seemingly dissolve all boundaries between the self and the object world. Since many of these artists had also read Suzuki, they came to associate psychedelic hallucination with the enlightenment of Zen. Reliable authorities such as Alan Watts and Gary Snyder made favorable comparisons between the reality-shattering experience of the psychedelic and the awakening to the Buddha mind. Timothy Leary, the Harvard psychologist who became a counterculture legend as the spokesman for psychedelic experience, referred to the effects of LSD as a "drug-induced

Figure 8.1. Alan Watts in his office at Druid Heights, Muir Woods California, 1972. Photo by Margo Moore, courtesy of Mark Watts.

satori."[6] For many psychedelic visionaries, Zen provided the perfect vocabulary with which to describe hallucination as a mode of religious experience.

As Zen increasingly became the spiritual rationale for all forms of avant-garde experimentation, up to and including recreational drug use, a backlash against it began to grow. Even Watts and Suzuki, who had done so much to popularize Zen, began to wonder if it had not become *too* popular. In 1958 Watts wrote an essay called "Phony Zen, Square Zen, and Zen," in which he took the Beats to task for their false identification of pleasure-seeking with enlightenment. Suzuki criticized the Beats, too, writing in 1958 that "they have probably not yet tapped the headspring of creativity." "They are struggling, still rather superficially," he wrote, "against 'democracy,' bourgeois conformity, economic respectability, conventional middle class consciousness, and other cognate virtues and vices of mediocrity." He emphatically denied that this kind of bohemianism was true Zen. "They have not yet passed," Suzuki argued, "through their experiences of humiliation and affliction and, I may add, revelation."[7] As for the psychedelic connection, its "obituary" was published in the pages of the *Eastern Buddhist* in 1971, five years after the U.S. government criminalized the use of LSD and every other known hallucinogenic substance. The essays of leading Zen luminaries, including Suzuki and Watts, concluded that the use of psychedelics was not a path to enlightenment but rather quite possibly a path to disorientation and psychosis. With this judgment, the divorce between the true Zen of religious awakening and the phony Zen of psychedelia was made final.

Freed from its brief, notorious association with psychedelics and the "criminal element" of the drug-using youth movement, American Zen in the early 1970s branched off into a two distinct paths of respectability. The first was a flowering of academic Zen studies, which produced an abundance of fine scholarship, in both the modern and postmodern critical veins, and drew the attention of serious students to the literature of the Zen masters themselves rather than just the learned but one-sided commentaries of D. T. Suzuki. Academic Zen scholars since the 1970s have made a point of distancing themselves from Suzuki, turning instead to the interpretations of more "authentic" scholar-monks, such as the modern Zen master Hu Shih, and engaging in a wide range of critical studies of the primary sources of the Chinese and Japanese masters.

The other development in mainstream Zen was the consolidation and expansion on Zen's familiar modern role as an alternative spiritual path for educated middle-class people who for various reasons had left the religious traditions of their upbringing. This Western movement ran parallel to a revival of Zen lay practice among postwar middle-class Japanese, many of whom came to appreciate Zen, ironically, as a result of its popularity in the United States. Monasteries in Japan began to offer Zen retreats for busy corporate "salarymen," defining a new role for the monastic community in secular postwar Japan. Celebrated Zen masters such as the Korean monk Seung Sahn and the Japanese abbot Shunryu Suzuki (no relation to D. T.) moved to the United States, becoming directors of influential Zen centers and serving as capable mentors for a new generation of modern dharma seekers. From the 1970s onward, Zen study centers were established worldwide, particularly in the West, catering to the spiritual aspirations of a large and diverse body of disciples. While many of these students entered the path of ordination to the Zen priesthood, including a number of women such as master Maurine Stuart, most "did" Zen as a form of self-improvement or therapy, working Zen meditation and well-practiced "awareness" into their busy lives.

During the years of the international postwar "Zen boom," Japan recovered its prosperity and sense of confidence and exported an expanding quantity of manufactured goods to the world. As Western children watched Ultra-man and Speed Racer on television and Western students took courses in Japanese studies in college, their political leaders watched with admiration and concern as Japan rose to economic superpower status. By the 1980s, Japanese culture had almost become a part of America's own cultural landscape, and Zen became something of a household word—even if people were still not entirely sure what it was. A good case in point may be seen in the phenomenal *Zen and the Art of Motorcycle Maintenance,* by Robert Pirsig, a philosophical memoir that capitalized on the familiarity of the average American with the word *Zen* and the promise that it might have some deep wisdom to offer about the concerns of everyday life.

Pirsig's modern classic has little to do with either Zen or motorcycle maintenance, but it does provide an interesting meditation on the divided nature of Western consciousness and traces the origins of the split back to the earliest days of Greek philosophy. The book's popularity may have something to do with the fact that even for educated westerners the philosophy of Aristotle is often just as foreign and exotic as Zen, and the author is able to connect contemporary alienation with some of the oldest debates in the Western tradition. Pirsig brings Zen into the narrative as a paradigm for nondualism and uses the motorcycle as a kind of high-tech *kōan*. He suggests that the split between aesthetic romanticism and scientific rationalism (is the motorcycle a "groovy" means of adventure and excitement or just a "square" machine made out of chains, tappets, and cylinders?) needs to be transcended in good Buddhist fashion in order to restore sanity to our civilization.

The millions of readers who have turned this book into a classic of postwar literature have proved that Zen, whether strictly defined or not, provides a useful frame for discussing any kind of ideological, political, or social divide and offers hope that it may ultimately be resolved. In the final analysis, if we wanted to identify Zen's chief contribution to modern consciousness, it may be just this. Zen looks at the fixed pronouncements of objective reality and says there is more there than meets the eye, yet it does so from a fresh, outside perspective that may hold more appeal than similar statements emerging from Western thought and religion. Zen has also allowed modern people to think beyond the confines of conventional categories, holding out the promise that there may be some common transcendental ground—something that the modern political, economic, and social systems have arguably been conspicuously poor at doing.

Looking at Zen in its various mainstream modern functions (as a critique of constructed order, a means of embracing dichotomy, and an agent for transformation), we can only wonder what the latest spin of the popular Zen wheel will bring to the long process of historical cross-cultural dialogue. I am referring to punk Zen, or hardcore Zen, the latest and greatest doctrine of nondoctrine, popularized by such edge-running gurus as Brad Warner and Noah Levine in their books *Hardcore Zen: Punk Rock, Monster Movies, and the Truth about Reality,* and *Dharma Punx: A Memoir,* respectively. This genre of Zen speaks forcefully to a new generation of alienated people, offering them a provocative, even creative way to frame their dissatisfaction with society by helping them deal with the fact that reality is "all there is" and it is often unpleasant. From a religious standpoint, though, punk Zen provides little in the way of spiritual comfort or metaphysical satisfaction. Beyond its dismissal of authority, its celebration of the self, and its admonitions to accept the world as it is, punk Zen has little wisdom to impart and rejects even the idea of enlightenment, framing it as an unrealistic, or even false, goal. Punk Zen may very well be an accurate expression of the disaffection of today's youth, but—and this brings us to our original question—is it really Zen? If not, what, after all, *is* Zen?

We set out on this narrative journey by defining Zen as Buddhist meditation. We then followed this specific Zen from its historical origins through the centuries, identifying a variety of intellectual, social, and cultural effects. What we have learned, hopefully, is that while Zen is not impossible to define, it certainly does resist any attempt at definition in a tidy or self-contained way. It may well be that this fluidity is precisely what has preserved Zen as a religious and cultural idea for so many years and under so many different historical circumstances. Perhaps the easier it is to pin something down, the less flexible and survivable it may be.

As you finish this booklet, I would encourage you to consult the "Suggestions for Further Reading" and take up this question in more depth. It may become a great lifelong hobby if not a genuine obsession! In the final analysis, we can probably say that any religious impulse that has survived for 2,500 years, crossed the entire globe, and stood witness to the rise and fall of empires and civilizations is likely to be around for a very long time.

Glossary

Absolute nothingness: Similar or equivalent to *sunyata*, or "the void." The term appears in Japanese Zen, particularly in the philosophy of Nishida Kitarō, where it also refers to the final end of the process of world history.

Arhat: In Buddhism, a person who has attained a high degree of spiritual development, sometimes translated as "saint."

Awakening: The state of realization attained by the Buddha during his enlightenment; "awakening" brought the Buddha to the knowledge of the Four Noble Truths. (Sanskrit, *samadhi*; Japanese, *satori*)

Buddha: The "enlightened one," the historical figure of Siddartha Gautama (ca. 563–483 BCE).

Bodhisattva: "Buddha-to-be," a person who is ready for full enlightenment but postpones nirvana for the sake of helping others attain salvation.

Chan: The Chinese word for *dhyāna*, "meditation."

Dharma: "Law," "doctrine" or "truth." The term is sometimes interpreted as "entities" or "identities," in which case it refers specifically to the inherent quality of phenomena in the three-dimensional object world.

Dhyāna: Meditation, the core practice of the Zen Buddhist tradition. (in Chinese, *Chan*; in Japanese, *Zen*).

Eightfold Path: An outline of Buddhist practice that enables one to overcome desire and thus overcome suffering, as indicated in the Four Noble Truths. The Eightfold Path consists of: (1) Right belief; (2) Right intention; (3) Right speech; (4) Right action; (5) Right Livelihood; (6) Right Endeavor; (7) Right Mindfulness; and (8) Right Meditation.

Enlightenment: The state one experiences in the attainment of Buddhahood. It denotes liberation from the cycle of birth and rebirth and the condition of human suffering. (in Sanskrit, *bodhi*)

Four Noble Truths: (1) Life is suffering; (2) suffering is caused by desire; (3) the cessation of desire leads to the cessation of suffering; (4) the Eightfold Path leads to the cessation of desire.

Karma: in Hinduism and Buddhism, the idea that the quality of one's deeds will create an effect drawing one back to successive incarnations in order to fulfill a life-destiny

Kōan: A paradox or riddle on which a Zen Buddhist meditates in order to break free of the trap of conventional thinking. This helps the seeker attain awakening.

Mahāyāna: The "Greater Vehicle," a school of Buddhist thought that began to emerge in the first generations after the Buddha's passing. It is generally thought to be a more inclusive, universal, and salvation-based form of Buddhism than the Theravada school.

Nirvana: "Extinction," symbolized by the image of "blowing out" a candle. Nirvana is the ultimate goal of Buddhist practice as it liberates the seeker from the necessity of rebirth.

Prajñāpāramitā: "Perfection of wisdom," the state of all knowing attained by the Buddha during his awakening. It is also is the name of a stream of Buddhist philosophy and its accompanying genre of sutras in the Mahāyāna tradition.

Samadhi: see *Awakening.*

Satori: A Japanese term that describes the experience of attaining "awakening" or "understanding" after "successful" Zen practice. Not to be confused with "nirvana," although the initial experience of satori is usually a necessary preliminary for attaining nirvana.

Sramana: Ascetic, world-renouncing teachers who lived in India at the time of the Buddha.

Sunyata: "The void," the state of emptiness attained by the Buddha during his awakening, when he realized that all objects of the world and mind are illusions.

Sutra: A Buddhist text or scripture.

Theravada: A Buddhist tradition named for the Theravadin, or "elders," the first disciples of the Buddha. Denoting a tradition that favors asceticism and monastic living, the term often appears in contrast to the rival Mahāyāna tradition. Theravada was the first Buddhist "school," and it is still believed by its adherents to represent the most correct Buddhist lifestyle.

Zazen: "sitting meditation." An essential practice of Zen Buddhism, modeled on the practice of the Buddha's own sitting in meditation as he waited for enlightenment.

Zen: The Japanese rendition of the word *dhyāna*, "meditation."

NOTES

CHAPTER 1

[1] Alan W. Watts, *The Way of Zen* (New York: Vintage Books, 1957), xii.

[2] David Schillers, *The Little Zen Companion* (New York: Workman Publishing, 1994), i.

[3] Masao Abe, *Zen and Western Thought*, ed. William R. LaFleur (Honolulu: University of Hawai'i Press, 1985), 4 (emphasis in the original).

[4] D. T. Suzuki, *The Essentials of Zen Buddhism*, ed. Bernard Phillips (New York: E. P. Dutton, 1962), 8.

[5] Ibid.

CHAPTER 2

[1] According the "three body doctrine" (Trikaya) of Buddhism, the Buddha exists as an historical person, a glorified exalted personage, and a metaphysical principle. Thus there are, spread through eternity, many different manifestations of the Buddha. It is not a contradiction that the Buddha in the form of an elephant was able to assist in the conception of the historical Buddha. By way of an analogy, however imprecise, we can compare this to God, the Holy Spirit of the Christian Trinity, assisting in the conception of God, the "Son" in the New Testament.

[2] The term *dharma* is generally used to mean "law" or "doctrine," and it refers in Buddhist literature to the Buddha's teaching of righteousness as universal moral Truth.

[3] Zenkei Shibayama, ed. *The Mumonkan* (Gateless Gate), case 6, The Buddha's Flower. Translated by Sumiko Kudo (New York: Harper and Row, 1974), 59.

CHAPTER 3

[1] Compilations of traditional Zen *kōan* may be found in a number of sources. Two of the more widely consulted are the *Biyan Lu*, or *Blue Cliff Record* (1125), and *Mumonkan*, or *Gateless Gate* (1228). See "Suggestions for Further Reading" for bibliographic information.

[2] Heinrich Dumoulin, *A History of Zen Buddhism* (Boston: Beacon Press, 1969), 54.

[3] Watts, *The Way of Zen*, 3.

[4] D. T. Suzuki, *The Essentials of Zen Buddhism* (New York: E. P. Dutton, 1962), 117.

[5] According to popular tradition he spent so long in sitting meditation that his arms and legs fell off. A related legend explains why most paintings depict him with large, intensely focused eyes. As the story goes, he became so angry with himself for falling asleep while trying to meditate that he cut off his eyelids.

[6] See Watts, *The Way of Zen*, 87.

[7] D. T. Suzuki, ed., *The Manual of Zen Buddhism* (New York: Grove Press, 1935), 82.

[8] Heinrich Dumoulin, *Zen Enlightenment: Origins and Meaning* (New York: Weatherhill, 1979), 44.

CHAPTER 4

[1] The term *dharma*, in addition to being defined as "law," "truth," or "doctrine," is also used to refer to entities or identities, in other words, the substantial qualities of phenomena in the object world.

[2] Avalokitesvara, the "lord who looks down," is also known as the bodhisattva of divine compassion. Known as Guanyin in China, and Kannon in Japan, Avalokitesvara is one of the best-known and widely revered bodhisattvas in the Mahāyāna pantheon.

[3] The five *skhandas* are traditionally identified as physical form, sensation, perception, will, and consciousness.

[4] Suzuki, *Manual of Zen Buddhism*, 26.

[5] Ibid., 27.

[6] Ibid., 58.

[7] Ibid., 64.

[8] Ibid., 52.

[9] Ibid., 50.

[10] Chang Chung Yuan, trans., *Original Teachings of Ch'an Buddhism: Selected from the Transmission of the Lamp* (New York: Pantheon Books, 1969), 5

[11] Ibid., 6.

[12] Ibid., 20.

CHAPTER 5

[1] Robert H. Sharf, "The Zen of Japanese Nationalism," *History of Religions* 33, no. 1 (August,1993): 6. In this article, Buddhist scholar Robert Sharf explains and critiques the tendency of many twentieth-century students of Zen to equate Zen Buddhism with Japan, leaving the false impression that Zen "is the essence of Japanese culture, and the key to the unique qualities of the Japanese race."

[2] Dumoulin, *A History of Zen Buddhism*, 133.

[3] Shitou, *The Identity of Relative and Absolute*, trans. Zen Center of Los Angeles, accessed at http://villagezendo.org/practice/sutras-and-gathas/relative-and-absolute/

[4] Consult "Suggestions for Further Reading" for bibliographic information.

CHAPTER 6

[1] D. T. Suzuki, *Zen and Japanese Culture* (Tokyo: Charles E. Tuttle, 1959), 69.

[2] Suzuki, *Manual of Zen Buddhism*, 150.

[3] Suzuki, *Zen and Japanese Culture*, 355.

[4] Yoshida Kenkō, *Essays in Idleness: The Tsurzuregusa of Kenkō*, trans. Donald Keene (New York: Columbia University Press, 1967), 70.

CHAPTER 7

[1] Hakuin, "The Song of Meditation," in *A First Zen Reader*, trans. Trevor Leggett (Tokyo: Charles E. Tuttle, 1960), 67.

[2] Rick Fields, *How the Swans Came to the Lake: A Narrative History of Buddhism in America* (Boston: Shambala, 1992), 126.

[3] Christmas Humphreys, *Zen Buddhism* (London: William Heinemann, 1949; reprint, London: Diamond Books, 1996), 139.

[4] Ibid., 137.

[5] Ruth Fuller Sasaki, quoted in Fields, *How the Swans Came to the Lake,* 205.

CHAPTER 8

[1] Christopher Ives, "Ethical Pitfalls in Imperial Zen and Nishida Philosophy," in *Rude Awakenings: Zen, the Kyoto School, and the Question of Nationalism*, ed. James W. Heisig and John C. Maraldo (Honolulu: University of Hawai'i Press, 1995), 18.

[2] Eric Cunningham, *Hallucinating the End of History: Nishida, Zen, and the Psychedelic Eschaton* (Bethesda: Academica Press, 2007), 302.

[3] Suzuki, *The Essentials of Zen Buddhism*, 371.

[4] Thomas Merton, "D. T. Suzuki: The Man and His Work," in *A Zen Life: D. T. Suzuki Remembered*, ed. Masao Abe (New York Weatherhill, 1986), 121.

[5] Jack Kerouac, *Some of the Dharma* (New York: Penguin, 1999), ix.

[6] Timothy Leary, quoted in Jay Stevens, *Storming Heaven: LSD and the American Dream* (New York: Atlantic Monthly Press, 1987), 158.

[7] Suzuki, *The Essentials of Zen Buddhism*, 373.

Suggestions for Further Reading

Abe, Masao. Introduction to *An Inquiry into the Good*, by Nishida Kitarō. New Haven and London: Yale University Press, 1990.

————. "Nishida's Philosophy of Place." *International Philosophical Quarterly* 28, no. 4 (December 1988): 354–71.

————. *A Study of Dōgen: His Philosophy and Religion*. Steven Heine, ed. Albany: State University of New York Press, 1992.

Abe, Masao, ed. *A Zen Life: D. T. Suzuki Remembered*. New York: Weatherhill, 1986.

Austin, James H. *Zen and the Brain: Toward an Understanding of Meditation*. Boston: Massachusetts Institute of Technology Press, 1998.

Cleary, Thomas and J. C. Cleary, trans. *The Blue Cliff Record*. Boston: Shambhala, 2005.

Dumoulin, Heinrich. *A History of Zen Buddhism*. Trans. Paul Peachey. Boston: Beacon Press, 1963.

————. *Zen Buddhism: A History*. Vol. 2: *Japan*. Trans. James W. Heisig and Paul Knitter. New York: Macmillan, 1990.

Ellwood, Robert S., ed. *Zen in American Life and Letters*. Malibu: Undena Publications, 1987.

Fields, Rick. *How the Swans Came to the Lake: A Narrative History of Buddhism in America*. Boulder: Shambala, 1981.

Heisig, James W., and John C. Maraldo, eds. *Rude Awakenings: Zen, the Kyoto School, and the Question of Nationalism*. Honolulu: University of Hawai'i Press, 1994.

Humphreys, Christmas. "Dr. D. T. Suzuki and Zen Buddhism in Europe." In *A Zen Life: D. T. Suzuki Remembered*, ed. Abe Masao, 81–89. New York: Weatherhill, 1986.

————. *Zen Buddhism*. London: William Heinemann, 1949; reprint, London: Diamond Books, 1996.

Jackson, Phil. *Sacred Hoops: The Spiritual Lessons of a Hardwood Warrior*. New York: Hyperion Books, 1996.

Kapleau, Philip. "Strategic Occidentalism: Meiji Buddhists at the World's Parliament of Religions." *Buddhist-Christian Studies*. Vol. 11 (1991): 37–55.

————. *The Three Pillars of Zen*. New York: Weatherhill, 1965.

Kerouac, Jack. *Some of the Dharma*. New York: Penguin, 1999.

————. *The Dharma Bums*. New York: Penguin, 1986, (reprint of 1958 Viking Press hardcover).

Ketelaar, James Edward. *Of Heretics and Martyrs in Meiji Japan: Buddhism and Its Persecution*. Princeton: Princeton University Press, 1990.

Kitagawa, Joseph M. *Religion in Japanese History*. New York: Columbia University Press, 1990.

Leggett, Trevor, ed. *A First Zen Reader*. Tokyo: Charles E. Tuttle, 1960.

Levine, Noah. *Dharma Punx: A Memoir*. San Francisco: Harper, 2003.

McRae, John R. "Oriental Verities on the American Frontier: The 1893 World's Parliament of Religions and the Thought of Masao Abe." *Buddhist Christian Studies*. Vol. 11 (1991): 7–35.

Merton, Thomas. "D. T. Suzuki: The Man and His Work." In *A Zen Life: D. T. Suzuki Remembered,* ed. Abe Masao, 121–26. New York: Weatherhill, 1986.

————. *Zen and the Birds of Appetite*. New York: New Directions, 1968.

Pirsig Robert M. *Zen and the Art of Motorcycle Maintenance*. New York: Bantam, 1974.

Shaku, Sōyen. [Sōen]. *Zen for Americans*. Trans. D. T. Suzuki. New York: Dorset, 1987.

Sharf, Robert. "Whose Zen? Zen Nationalism Revisited." In *Rude Awakenings: Zen, the Kyoto School, and the Question of Nationalism*, ed. James W. Heisig and John C. Maraldo, 40–51. Honolulu: University of Hawai'i Press, 1994.

————. "The Zen of Japanese Nationalism." *History of Religions*. Vol. 33 (August 1993): 1–43.

Shibayama, Zenkei. *Zen Comments on the Momonkan* (Gateless Gate). Translated by Sumiko Kudo. New York: Harper and Row, 1974.

Stevens, Jay. *Storming Heaven: LSD and the American Dream*. New York: Atlantic Monthly Press, 1987.

Suzuki, Daisetsu [D. T.]. "An Autobiographical Account." In *A Zen Life: D. T. Suzuki Remembered*, ed. Abe Masao, 13–26. New York: Weatherhill, 1986.

————. *The Essentials of Zen Buddhism: An Anthology of the Writings of Daisetz T. Suzuki*. Ed. and with an introduction by Bernard Phillips. New York: E. P. Dutton, 1962.

————. ed. *Manual of Zen Buddhism*. New York: Grove Press, 1935.

————. *The Outlines of Mahāyāna Buddhism*. New York: Schocken Books, 1963.

————. *Shin shūkyō ron* (A new treatise on the meaning of religion) [1896]. In *Suzuki Daisetsu Zenshū* (The complete works of Suzuki Daisetsu), vol. 23, 1–147. Tokyo: Iwanami Shoten. 1969.

————. *Zen and Japanese Culture*. New York: Bollingen Foundation, 1959.

Suzuki, D. T., Erich Fromm, and Richard DeMartino, *Zen Buddhism and Psychoanalysis*. New York: Grove Press, 1960.

Suzuki, D. T., et al. "Drugs and Buddhism: A Symposium," *Eastern Buddhist* 4, no. 2 (October 1971): 128–33.

Thurman, Robert A. F. *The Holy Teaching of Vimalakirti: A Mahayana Scripture*. University Park: Pennsylvania State University Press, 2001.

Victoria, Brian A. [Daizen]. *Zen at War*. New York: Weatherhill, 1997.

Warner, Brad. *Hardcore Zen: Punk Rock, Monster Movies, and the Truth about Reality*. Boston: Wisdom Publications, 2003.

Watts, Alan W. *The Way of Zen*. New York: Vintage Books, 1957.

————. *This Is It and Other Essays on Zen and Spiritual Experience*. New York: Pantheon Books, 1958.

CPSIA information can be obtained at www.ICGtesting.com
Printed in the USA
BVOW071257270912

301473BV00003B/1/P